Puppy Training

The Guide Dogs Way

RINGPRESS

Julia Barnes

Guide Dogs

ACKNOWLEDGEMENTS

The publisher would like to thank The Guide Dogs for the Blind Association for its help and co-operation, and particularly the many puppy walkers who so generously gave their time and shared their experiences.

The Question of Gender
The 'he' pronoun is used throughout this book in favour of the rather impersonal 'it', but no gender bias is intended.

Published by Ringpress Books Ltd,
a division of Interpet Publishing,
Vincent Lane, Dorking,
Surrey, RH4 3YX, UK.
Tel: 01306 873822   Fax: 01306 876712
email: sales@interpet.co.uk

Designed by Sarah Williams
First Published 2004

ISBN-13 978-186054-209-1

Printed in China through Printworks Int. Ltd.
0 9 8 7 6 5

CONTENTS

FOREWORD

No matter why you own dogs, whether it is to show, work, or just as a pet, there are two qualities common to all: that they should be as free of health problems as is possible and that they should be temperamentally sound.

No dog is absolutely perfect in every respect but, with a little effort, it is possible to get quite close!

A good dog is the result of careful, selective breeding and its subsequent upbringing during the pups formative first months.

Since 1957, Guide Dogs in the UK has successfully operated a Breeding and Puppy Walking Scheme which has produced many thousands of puppies which have gone on to make guides.

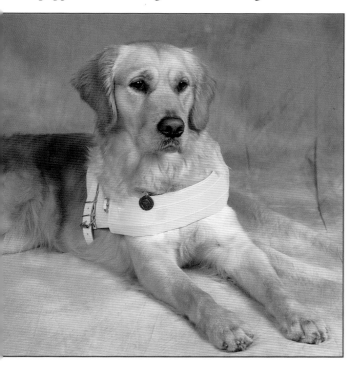

This has involved keeping very strict records of all the dogs bred, being brave and honest enough to acknowledge and act on problems, as well as identifying practises which result in success.

Dog breeding consists of three components. The first is the science of breeding, which includes a knowledge of genetics, pedigrees, hereditary problems and much more. The next is the art of looking at, and accurately assessing a dog. This is sometimes called stockmanship. Finally, nature dictates that luck will play a big part in deciding the makeup of a litter of pups. However, this should be regarded as part of the fun of breeding dogs.

Rearing a puppy will be quite hard work if it is done properly, but it should be fun as well. No matter what a dog is acquired for, your life together should be a pleasure.

Guide Dogs are very pleased to have worked with the author on this book. As a charity, which is totally supported by the public, it is right that we should share our experiences and observations. We breed and then place over one thousand puppies a year on the Puppy Walking Schemes throughout the country. Each is monitored very carefully and over the many years and we have learned a lot of lessons.

Despite this we must never get complacent, as it is important to admit that we do not know everything. There is always something waiting to catch us out.

I should quote the late Derek Freeman MBE who was Guide Dogs Breeding Manager for over twenty seven years. On his retirement he got things into perspective when he said with real feeling: "Pity about that. I was starting to get the hang of this breeding game!"

Owning a dog need not be complicated. It is mostly a matter of common sense and, I suggest, a good sense of humour!

Dogs enrich all our lives in so many ways. Even those who do not own them enjoy the protection given by police dogs, or cannot fail to be affected by the sight of dogs searching for disaster victims. On our streets they act as guides, assist the deaf and people with other disabilities.

Dogs are vitally important companions for thousands of humans. No matter what their purpose, each and every dog should be bred and reared well.

I hope you will enjoy the contents of this book and that the many observations, all based on years of practical experience, will help you have a long and relatively trouble-free life with this great friend of ours… the dog.

Neil Ewart
Breeding Quality Co-ordinator,
The Guide Dogs for the Blind Association.

CHAPTER ONE

THE PERFECT DOG

The aim of every dog owner is to have a perfect dog: beautiful to look at, well behaved in all situations, and a loving, affectionate companion. When you go to choose a puppy, and he first arrives in his new home, there seems no reason why these goals should not be realised. You are ready to give the time to training the pup, and he seems happy to oblige. How could anything go wrong?

The answer is: all too easily, and for a wide variety of different reasons. Sometimes, a family has not given enough thought to the breed of dog that is most likely to suit their lifestyle. A dog may prove to be too big and boisterous to live in a tiny apartment, or he may be too small and delicate to put up with the hurly-burly of hectic family life.

Everyone starts with the intention of giving endless time to training and socialising a pup, but after an enthusiastic start, too many people find they haven't got enough time to do the job properly. Training classes are missed, and it seems easier to leave the dog at home rather than slowing down by taking him on a trip to the shops.

Then there are the agonies of adolescence when even the best-behaved dog takes a turn for the worse. Your authority is challenged, and you need endless patience to guide your pup through his teenage phase.

Reading this, it may seem as if the dream of having a perfect dog is unattainable, but this is far from the case. You may not reach total perfection – but if you follow certain guidelines, you can get very close.

GUIDE DOG PUPPIES

Guide dogs, who take on the task of guiding a blind or partially sighted person, face one of the hardest jobs a dog can be expected to undertake.

• A guide dog works in heavy traffic, moving among crowds of people, ignoring all distractions.

It takes time to train and socialise a puppy.

9

A guide dog must be prepared to meet many challenges in his daily work.

- He must listen to commands from his owner, but should have the intelligence and initiative to think for himself if a situation demands it.
- A guide dog must work with intense concentration when he is guiding his owner, but then must be prepared to settle quietly when he is not required.
- He must be friendly and out-going, accepting the attention of everyone he meets.
- He must be a loyal and loving companion.

As a wish list goes, this seems virtually impossible to achieve. But The Guide Dogs for the Blind Association has an amazing success rate. Currently, three out of every four pups it breeds and rears qualify as guide dogs. What is the secret of its success?

Back in the early 1960s, Guide Dogs struggled to find enough dogs who were suitable to train. It relied on adults donated to The Association, and, as a result, there was little consistency over the type of dog they had to work with. It was quickly realised that there was far more chance of producing an adult that was suitable for training if it was correctly reared as a puppy.

The puppy walking scheme, pioneered by Derek Freeman, proved to be a major breakthrough. Labrador Retrievers, Golden Retrievers and German Shepherd Dogs were the most successful breeds for guide dog work, so sound, typical pups from these breeds were bought and then placed in the homes of puppy walkers. The volunteer family was given the responsibility of rearing and training the pup from six weeks to around 12 months, which is when advanced training starts.

This method of rearing has proved enormously successful, and The Guide Dogs for the Blind Association now has 1,100 puppy walkers. There are a number of huge benefits associated with puppy walking:
- The puppies are reared in a family environment, and learn to accept their status

within the human 'pack'.
- They are exposed to the outside world from an early age, and learn to accept and adapt to a wide variety of situations.
- Training is a part of everyday life, and the pups thrive on the mental stimulation this provides.

Puppy walkers are visited regularly by a puppy walking supervisor, and this means that a close check can be kept on each puppy's progress. Help and advice can be given at an early stage if any problems arise.

The number of pups going through to formal training as guide dogs increased dramatically as the puppy walking scheme grew. But there was one more important step to be taken before The Association achieved the success rate it needed.

The breeding programme was launched, and this meant that the best dogs and bitches could be selected for breeding. For the first time, experts could look at the physical characteristics, the mental aptitude, and the temperament that were needed for guide dog work, and then set out to find the dogs that were most likely to pass on these desirable traits.

Today, The Guide Dogs for the Blind Association has 50 stud dogs and 250 brood bitches, and produces around 1,000 puppies every year.

FORGING A LINK

Successful breeding and rearing is the result of experience spread over many years. The Association can now go back four to five generations, tracing the history of every dog it has bred. Information is stored on computer from the moment a dog is born through to its eventual demise. This is a luxury not afforded to any other breeders, as those selling pups commercially are dependent on puppy buyers

The breeding programme has had a big impact on the success rate of dogs going forward for formal, advanced training.

If you put in the work training your puppy, you will be rewarded by having an adult dog you are proud to own.

contacting them – and the information supplied being accurate.

The depth of experience and expertise that has been developed both in breeding and through the puppy walking scheme is unique. These methods now have worldwide recognition, and have been used as a model for Dogs for the Disabled, Canine Partners, and Hearing Dogs for the Deaf. The police and other services also rear their puppies the Guide Dog way.

THE PET OWNER

If you have just bought a puppy as a pet, you may well think that the way you rear your pup bears little relation to what the professionals are doing. In fact, there should be absolutely no difference.

Neil Ewart, who has worked for Guide Dogs for more than 30 years, specialising in breeding and rearing puppies, says: "Regardless of whether you are rearing a guide dog, a dog for the disabled, a police dog, or a pet dog, the methods are exactly the same. The aim is to select a puppy with a good family background, and to give him a sound, all-round education that will equip him for his future life."

DOGS IN THE COMMUNITY

Owning a dog is not the simple business that it used to be when no one took much notice of whether you had a dog or not. Today, there is a strong anti-dog feeling in the community, and increasingly there are restrictions on where you can take your dog and the places where free-running exercise is permitted.

For this reason, it is imperative that all dog owners produce model canine citizens, who behave in a manner that is socially acceptable. A badly behaved dog, or a poorly socialised dog who appears aggressive or fearful, gives the anti-dog lobby all the ammunition it needs to place further limits on dog owners. The list of banned breeds will grow, and it will become increasingly difficult to take a dog out in public places.

THE RIGHT START

Training your dog to be well behaved, adaptable and reliable must be the goal of every responsible dog owner. Every breed is different, every dog is an individual, and every owner has different expectations and ambitions. However, the broad principles of rearing a puppy are identical.

Drawing on the expertise and experience of The Guide Dogs for the Blind Association, this book provides a comprehensive programme of training and socialisation, which will give you and your dog every chance of success. Hard work and commitment are needed on both sides, but the effort you put in for the first 12 months of your dog's life will pay dividends for the rest of your time together.

Every dog must be trained to be a good canine citizen.

CHAPTER TWO

THE CHOICE IS YOURS

Taking on a dog is a huge commitment, and you will need to give the matter a lot of thought before taking the plunge. You may not have owned a dog before, you may be replacing a much-loved companion, or you may be adding another member to a growing canine family. In all cases, you must resist the temptation of rushing out and buying the first pup you come across.

Hopefully, you will be living with your dog for the next 12 years or so, and you will want a partnership that is going to work. Be honest with yourself, assessing how much time you can give to your dog, how much space you have, and what will work within your family set-up.

There are so many breeds, all different shapes, sizes and temperaments. Shops are brimming with excellent books describing in detail the common breeds, plus many rarer examples. So, spend as much time as possible finding out about the breeds you are interested in.

Give thought to the following considerations:

SIZE

The breed you choose must fit in with the living accommodation that is available. Of course, a large breed, such as an Irish Wolfhound, can fit into a tiny apartment, but if you have limited space, particularly if you only have a very small garden, your workload – in terms of providing adequate exercise – will be a major consideration.

Remember, your dog also needs to fit into your car, so a St. Bernard and a two-seater sports car might not be the best combination!

On the other end of the scale, a tiny dog, such as a Chihuahua, or a delicate dog, such as an Italian Greyhound, would be a poor choice if you have a family with young children. The rough and tumble of family life is generally too much for these tinies.

A St. Bernard puppy is adorable – but you need to have the room to accommodate an adult.

EXERCISE

Taking your dog for a walk should be one of the great pleasures of owning a dog, but you must be realistic about planning a routine that you know you will be able to stick to.

There are many breeds that are content with a moderate amount of exercise, and that includes many of the larger breeds, such as the Greyhound, as well as the smaller Toy breeds.

If you have lots of time, and you enjoy walking, you can choose an active dog, such as a Border Collie, or one of the retrieving breeds, who will be more than happy to keep you company on day-long rambles.

COAT CARE

Some owners love grooming. They find it therapeutic, and feel it gives them a closer relationship with their dog. There are others who prefer a minimalist approach and a regular check and a quick brush down is all they have time for.

Make up your mind about grooming before you buy your puppy. It is all too easy to fall in love with a glamorous, longcoated breed, such as the Rough Collie, and then be burdened with a dog that you cannot care for properly.

TRAINING

Every dog needs to be trained, regardless of its size. A Yorkshire Terrier might not knock you flying if he jumps up, but he is still capable of making a great nuisance of himself unless he knows who is the boss.

Providing some degree of mental stimulation is also important, particularly with dogs that have a strong working instinct, such as the Border Collie.

Think twice before you take on a breed that has a dominant nature, such as a Rottweiler. This type of dog responds well to discipline, but you will need to spend a considerable amount of time working with your dog and establishing your authority.

CHOOSING A BREED

Every breed of dog is descended from the wolf – even though you may think a Poodle in show clip does not look very wolf-like! They retain many of the characteristics of their wild ancestor, which we will be examining in Chapter 5. However, through selective breeding, man has developed certain traits in order to produce dogs that are capable of carrying out specific tasks.

When you are weighing up the pros and cons of which breed to choose, it is important to research its working past. In most cases, this will have a big influence on the dog's needs and his temperament, even though he may not be bred from working lines.

GUNDOGS

All the breeds in this group were developed as shooting companions, specialising in the tasks required by a sporting owner.

- Spaniels were used to flush out game and to retrieve.
- Pointers and Setters were used to find and point or set game.

Believe it or not, the Poodle (like all other breeds) is descended from the wolf.

Wendy McPherson has puppy walked six Guide Dog puppies. Her seventh pup, Candy, is a Golden Retriever.

"I have always puppy walked Retriever breeds," said Wendy. "I have had three purebred Labradors, two Labrador-Retriever crosses, and a Golden Retriever.
On the whole, they have all been very calm, and they have been confident in all sorts of different situations.

"Labradors tend to chew more than Goldens – our house still bears the scars – but since I started using an indoor kennel, we have kept damage to a minimum. I keep the pup in an indoor kennel overnight for the first 3-4 months, and if I have to go out during the day, I would leave the pup in his indoor kennel."

Candy, Wendy's Golden Retriever pup, has still landed up in more than her fair share of trouble.

"She was the sort of puppy you had to watch all the time. She liked digging in the garden, and she was always getting hold of things she wasn't allowed. The worse time was when she swallowed a cloth, and she needed surgery to remove it.

"But since she has had her season, she has changed completely. She has calmed down, and she really is as good as gold."

Guide Dogs are so impressed with her temperament that she is being assessed as a potential brood birch.

"They want to see her now she's full grown, and then they will decide."

Wendy has puppy walked more males than females, but she does not have a particular preference.

"I found the bitches quite hard work just before they came into season. Probably the easiest dog I have had was King. He was a Golden Retriever, and I hardly knew I had him. From the moment he arrived, everything fell into place, and then he sailed through his training and qualified as a guide dog."

Wendy is now nearing the point when she will have to decide whether she takes on another puppy.

"I am in the process of persuading my husband," she said. "To be honest, the puppies become part of your life, and, even though they are hard work, I would be lost without one."

Candy: As good as gold.

- Retrievers were used to retrieve game on land and in water.
- All-round Gundogs, such as the German Shorthaired Pointer and the Hungarian Vizsla, were developed in Europe, and they are capable of carrying out all types of gundog work.

The unifying feature is that all these breeds must work closely with their owner in a controlled situation. It is because of this that gundogs are very biddable and easy to train. They are loyal and affectionate, and they love to work.

Retrieving breeds make up the vast majority of dogs used for guide dog work. Labradors are the most commonly used pure-bred dogs, followed by Golden Retrievers, though crosses between the two are the most successful of all. Flat Coated Retrievers and Curly Coated Retrievers are also suitable. Many of the other assistance dog charities, such as Dogs for the Disabled and Canine Partners, have also found that Retrievers are the best type of dog to choose.

If you want a lively, intelligent, affectionate dog that fits in well with family life, it may be that a Gundog is the type of dog that will suit you best. Find out about the characteristics of the different breeds in this group before making your choice.

The retrieving breeds, such as this Labrador Retriever, are intelligent and eager to please.

The Greyhound is bred to run – but he also likes to take life easy!

HOUNDS

This group includes the dogs that were bred to hunt, either by scent or by sight. The sighthounds, such as the Greyhound, the Afghan Hound and the Saluki, are fine, elegant dogs built to run at tremendous speed. Although these breeds love the chance to gallop at full stretch, they are also more than happy to take life easy on a sofa!

The scenthounds, which vary in size from the Bloodhound to the Dachshund, were developed to pick up a scent and follow it over a considerable distance. In most cases, these breeds have a lot of stamina and require regular exercise.

The common bond between the sighthounds and the scenthounds is that their inherited skills are very much part of their make-up. If a Basset Hound picks up a scent, or a Greyhound sights something he considers to be moving prey, there will be little chance of stopping them. Of course, these instincts can be diluted or channelled in more useful directions (see Chapter 5), but you should take them into consideration when making your choice.

TERRIERS

The breeds in this group were mostly used to go to ground after foxes and rabbits. The dogs needed to be brave and determined, yet small enough to go down a hole. These breeds, which include the Jack Russell, the Cairn Terrier and the Border Terrier, are tough little characters that like to lead an active life.

The Staffordshire Bull Terrier can be difficult to mix with other dogs.

The other type of terrier is descended from dogs that were used for bull-baiting and dog-fighting, as well as for catching rats. The Bull Terrier and the Staffordshire Bull Terrier are examples of these breeds. The barbaric sports these dogs were used for have long since been outlawed, and the breeds have found a new lease of life as loyal companions. However, the instinct to fight has not completely vanished, and this type of dog can be difficult to mix with other dogs.

PASTORAL

This group covers all the breeds that were developed to work with livestock. It includes the herding breeds, such as the Border Collie, the Rough Collie, and the Bearded Collie, as well as the short-legged Corgi. Generally, the Collie breeds are energetic dogs that require plenty to do. The Border Collie is the workaholic of the dog world, and thrives on an active, stimulating life. A small proportion of Border Collies and Border Collie crosses are used as guide dogs, and they are well suited to the more active owner.

The larger, heavier breeds, such as the Pyrenean Mountain Dog and the Maremma Sheepdog, were used to guard the flock. They are gentle, affectionate dogs, but, as their role demanded, they can be formidable when roused.

The German Shepherd Dog was used to herd and to guard the flock. It is the chosen breed for the police and other security services, but is also used as a guide dog. Approximately four per cent of the animals in the Guide Dogs training programme are German Shepherds. This is a highly intelligent breed that has great loyalty. However, a German Shepherd needs skilful handling to bring out the best in him, and is not a good choice unless you have the time to devote to him.

WORKING

This is a large group that covers all the working breeds that are not associated with herding. It includes the breeds with highly developed guarding instincts, such as the Mastiff, the Boxer and the Rottweiler. These are strong dogs, which have a

The Border Collie gets the vote for being the workaholic of the dog world.

The Rottweiler needs an experienced handler.

tendency to dominate. Although they make excellent companions, they need an experienced owner.

The sled dogs, such as the Siberian Husky and the Alaskan Malamute, are attractive, athletic dogs, built to work in harsh conditions for long periods. They do not adapt well to a pet home, unless you can provide the mental stimulation and the exercise they require.

TOY

The breeds in this group were bred specifically to be companions, and so they are very much 'people' dogs who love attention. In many cases, they were bred to be lap-sized, and so they include all the tinies of the dog world. This type of dog can be lively and spirited, but its size may mean it is better suited to a home without children – or where children are slightly older (over eight years).

The Cavalier King Charles Spaniel is the biggest representative, and will fit in well with family life, as well as being suitable for the more active owner.

Eunice Young has been a puppy walker for Guide Dogs for seven years, and she has worked with Labradors and Labrador-Golden Retriever crosses. Her first German Shepherd puppy, Cassidy, has qualified as a guide dog, and Eunice is now puppy walking her second Shepherd, called Toby. Eunice confesses that she has become a total convert to the breed.

"When I was first offered a Shepherd to puppy walk, I wasn't that keen. I had seen Shepherds out and about, and I always thought they were rather suspicious-looking dogs. But neither Cassidy nor Toby were like that. They both settled into the family straight away."

Eunice is married and has two teenage daughters, but Eunice takes on the main task of training and caring for the guide dog puppy.

"Our puppies have always responded to everyone in the family, but the Shepherds do tend to adopt one person. For example, we all went out the other evening, and Toby was on his own for an hour or so. When we got back, he took no notice of my husband; he wanted to greet me first. But on an ordinary day, when I am at home and my husband comes back from work, Toby makes a big fuss of him."

QUICK TO LEARN
Eunice has found both Shepherds quick to learn.

"They are clever dogs and pick things up very quickly – but they are quick at finding a way of wriggling out of doing the things they don't like. I use the lead as a sort of harness when Toby is pulling, and you would be amazed at how he can find his way out of it."

The only problem Eunice experienced during Cassidy's training was a slight awareness of traffic.

"He was a very laid-back dog, but when he was a puppy, he was a bit worried about traffic. I live on a busy road, so I used to sit on the wall outside my house and let him watch the traffic go by. He soon got over his concern."

Like all puppy walkers, Eunice devotes a lot of time to socialisation.

"Shepherds are very inquisitive, but they like to stand looking at something, working out what it is. In the early stages, I let the pup do this, and that seems to give them the confidence they need."

"Cassidy grew into a large, fine-looking dog, and Toby, at five months, is showing every sign of developing into a big dog.

"The only trouble I have is dealing with people's perceptions of Shepherds," says Eunice. "They see a great, big dog running up, and they get worried, particularly those who have small dogs. Shepherd puppies can be a bit rough when they are playing, and you have to make sure you keep control and the dog listens to you – even when he is doing something he wants to do."

Eunice has an ideal arrangement when it comes to socialising Toby with other dogs. Her sister-in-law, Debbie Coke, is also a Guide Dog puppy walker, and she is currently walking Toby's litter brother, Timber.

SHEPHERD BROTHERS
"When Cassidy went in for training, I took a break from puppy walking," says Eunice. "I thought the world of Cassidy, and it was hard to give him up. But Debbie persuaded me to carry on, so now we have the two Shepherd brothers. They love playing together, but we can also work on

their training when we go out."

Generally, Shepherds stay with their puppy walkers longer than most breeds, as they take longer to mature. In the majority of cases, they are ready for training when they are around 14 months. Then it will be time for Eunice to decide whether she will take on another Guide Dog puppy.

"I expect we'll carry on," she says, "as long as we get another Shepherd!"

Cassidy: He quickly settled into family life.

The Bulldog, a representative of the Utility breeds, is loving and affectionate – but not the easiest to train.

UTILITY

This is the group for all the breeds that don't fit into any other category. It includes breeds as diverse as the Dalmatian, the Bulldog, and the Poodle, so you will need to research each individual breed to find out its characteristics and requirements.

MIXED BREEDS

A crossbreed is a dog that has purebred parents of different breeds. Guide Dogs has found that crossing certain breeds, such as the Labrador and the Golden Retriever, produces outstanding results, combining the virtues of both breeds. Interestingly, the success rate drops off if two crossbreeds are mated, and so The Association always sticks with first-time crosses.

You may be offered a crossbreed, such as a Labrador-Collie cross, particularly if you go to a rescue shelter, and these dogs can make excellent companions. However, there is always a degree of uncertainty, as you cannot be sure which characteristics are likely to dominate.

A mongrel is a dog with parents of unknown ancestry, and there is no way of knowing how such a dog will turn out in terms of looks or temperament. There have been many wonderful 'Heinz 57' pets, but remember, as with any dog, there are no guarantees.

FINDING A BREEDER

When you have made the big decision as to which breed you would like to own, the next step is to find a breeder. Guide Dogs breeds virtually all its own puppies, but it still obtains around 100 a year from outside breeders, and therefore faces the same problems as the public in terms of finding a good source of quality puppies.

Many people find themselves filled with trepidation when they start to look for a new puppy to join the family. However, if you have decided on a pedigree puppy, there are some simple guidelines that can help you make the right decision.

The process is not dissimilar to buying a car. Decide on the make and model that best suits your lifestyle. Ask questions, and do not be afraid to get someone 'in the know' to view any pups you may be interested in.

The Labrador-Golden Retriever cross has proved highly successful for guide dog work.

The male (left) may be bigger and more powerful than the female (right).

WHERE TO START

There are a number of ways of finding a reputable breeder:

- Contact the Kennel Club for a list of breed clubs. Then get in touch with the secretary of the club in your area, and find out the names of breeders who have litters due, or who have puppies available.
- Go to a Championship dog show, and spend some time looking at the breed of your choice. If you see a type you like, talk to the exhibitor (after judging is finished). The dog may be home-bred, or you can find out which kennel it is from.
- If you live in the UK, visit the Discover Dogs show, or Crufts, where all breeds are represented and advice is freely available.
- Buy a specialist dog paper, and look at the classified adverts.
- Use the internet, and look at the websites of registered Kennel Club breeders. This will give you the opportunity to find out about the breeder's kennel and see photos of the dogs they have produced.
- If you are going for one of the more popular breeds, you may find that litters are advertised in your local paper. Make sure the litter is Kennel Club registered before proceeding any further, otherwise there is no guarantee that you are buying a pedigree puppy.

WHAT DO YOU WANT?

When you make contact with a breeder, make sure you fill them in on why you want to buy a puppy. It may seem obvious to you, but the breeder needs to find out if he/she has a suitable pup for the home on offer.

You may have any of the following preferences:

MALE OR FEMALE?

To a large extent, this is a matter of personal preference, but it is advisable to make up your mind before going to see the litter. In most breeds, the male will be slightly bigger than the female; in the large breeds, the male will be stronger and more powerful.

Many pet owners opt for a bitch – but remember that you will have to cope with her seasonal cycle, unless you plan to have her neutered (see page 116). A male may be more assertive in temperament, particularly during adolescence. Some males also develop a wanderlust, always on the look-out for bitches in season. This, and other related behaviour problems, can be solved by neutering (see page 116).

COAT AND COLOUR

You may have set your heart on a particular colour or coat type (depending on the breed). Obviously, this is purely an aesthetic concern, but if it is something you really want, you may have to wait until a suitable pup is available.

PET OR SHOW?

It is vital that you are honest with the breeder as to whether you plan to show your dog in the breed ring. A puppy with show potential must have the correct conformation, colour, coat type and markings if he is to be successful in the ring. He must move correctly, enjoy 'showing off', and not mind being handled.

A breeder can only sell a pup as a show prospect – there is no guarantee that he will mature into a top-class specimen of the breed. However, no self-respecting breeder, who has a reputation to guard, will want to sell a pet puppy and then see him exhibited in the ring. The pup may be ideal as a pet, but a pup sold on these terms may have a minor fault, such as a faulty marking, which makes him unsuitable for the show ring.

WORKING

If you have plans to work your dog, whether as a Gundog, a racing dog, in sheepdog trials, or in one of the competitive disciplines, such as Obedience, Agility, or Working Trials, you should go to a breeder that specialises in breeding working dogs. Again, there is no guarantee that your pup will excel in the activity you choose, but the chances are greatly enhanced if he inherits the working capabilities of his parents and grandparents.

FAMILY BACKGROUND

A pedigree puppy will inherit the characteristics of his breed in terms of what he looks like and the behavioural traits that have become cemented as a result of selective breeding. For example, a Labrador Retriever will inherit the instinct to retrieve, whereas a Greyhound will inherit the instinct to chase. This is not to say that every purebred Labrador will be a brilliant retriever, or that every Greyhound is going to win the Derby, but their genetic make-up means that they have a far greater chance of inheriting a breed-specific instinct.

There are also a number of general behavioural characteristics, which are inherited. These could be undesirable traits, such as fear or aggression, or they could be desirable traits, such as boldness or trainability.

If you plan to work your dog, you should go to a specialist breeder.

Research the pup's family background to find out about health, temperament and appearance. Pictured left to right: Walton (Guide Dog stud), Kresa (daughter – Guide Dog puppy in training), and Fay (Guide Dog brood).

There is a third area of inheritance, which is also of vital importance. There are a number of health conditions that are inherited directly from generation to generation. These include conditions that affect the dog's movement, such as hip dysplasia and elbow dysplasia, eyes conditions, such as progressive retinal atrophy, as well as a number of breed-specific disorders. For example, Dalmatians have a high incidence of inheriting deafness. A breeder must be 100 per cent confident that the dogs they use for breeding are not carrying the genes for any of these conditions.

Comments made over recent years suggesting that non-pedigree dogs are more likely to be free of hereditary health problems are a gross over-simplification. A reputable breeder of pedigree dogs will inform you if their lines have had problems, and they will have taken steps to eradicate any

inherited disorders.

When searching for your puppy, bear in mind that the perfect dog (or human!) has yet to be bred. It is inevitable that some problems, usually minor, will occur. It is an interesting fact that all humans carry at least three defective genes, which can be passed on to descendants. It is totally unrealistic to expect dogs to be any different!

The skill of the breeder lies not only in selecting the stud dog and the brood bitch that are most likely to complement each other. He or she must also research the family background of both prospective parents in order to find out as much as possible about the individual dogs in their line. In this way an assessment can be made of both animals, with the aim of cementing the good points, and eliminating the bad points in the resulting litter.

CHAPTER THREE

THE RIGHT START

Selecting breeding stock is a matter of prime importance. At Guide Dogs, temperament and health are viewed as top priorities. The bloodlines of prospective brood bitches and stud dogs are investigated for incidence of inherited disorders and specific behavioural traits. Character tests are also carried out to assess the individual dog's reactions to a variety of stimuli.

Animals selected for breeding must have the following qualities:

THE STUD DOG
- Looks right for the breed.
- Comes from known successful bloodlines.
- Is as free from known hereditary problems as is possible.
- Has had his eyes checked for inherited disorders.
- Has hip and elbow scores at an acceptable level. (There is a scheme for X-raying and scoring hips and elbows. Breed averages are published on an annual basis.)
- Has a good, sound temperament.
- Has not been over-used at stud.

THE BROOD BITCH
As above, and in addition:
- Must have a kind, equable temperament. In particular, she should not show worry/aggression when she is approached with her litter.
- She should not be used if she has real problems whelping first or subsequent litters.

INHERITED CHARACTERSTICS
There are some characteristics, both physical and temperamental, which are more likely to be inherited than others are. The heritability of a particular trait can vary from 1 to 100 per cent,

Stud dog Bruce: Great care is taken selecting Guide Dog breeding stock.

ON THE WRONG SCENT

"When you are assessing the temperament of a dog, it is sensible not to jump to conclusions," writes Neil Ewart, who has been closely involved in selecting breeding stock for The Guide Dogs for the Blind Association.

"A situation I faced a few years ago involved a nice Labrador bitch that I was training as a guide dog. She was quite advanced, and was being walked through the middle of Leamington Spa.

"Coming towards me was an elderly road sweeper, whom I had met many times, pushing a handcart that contained the rubbish he had collected from the pavement. As he approached, the dog started to back away. She seemed to be worried by the human rather than the cart, and got into a panic. This was very much out of character and she would not respond to verbal or physical encouragement. Even titbits had no effect! Rather than make matters worse, I decided to simply walk on and try to dismiss the incident from her mind.

"A few days later, I met the same man, with the same cart – and I was walking the same bitch. This time, there was absolutely no problem. I stopped to chat, and asked what he thought of the incident. 'Ah well,' he said, 'I think I know what was wrong. There was a dead cat in the cart, and I reckon she could smell it, and it frightened her.'

"That was surely the answer. My assumption that it was probably the old man himself that had somehow 'spooked' the bitch was wrong. She could smell something that upset her but could not see where it actually was. If I had not met the old man again, then the assumption that certain humans could upset her would have been put on the dog's record. "

There are some aspects of temperament that are more likely to be inherited than others.

depending on what is being studied. The following table has been compiled from various sources based on the experience of large-scale breeding kennels.

Characteristic	Inheritability
Litter size	10-20 per cent
Fertility	10-20 per cent
Temperament	30-50 per cent
Fear	46 per cent
Hip dysplasia	25-45 per cent
Panosteitis	13 per cent
(a condition causing lameness in puppies)	
Other features	40 per cent

There are some behavioural characteristics that seem to show up more in certain bloodlines. Guide Dogs would always avoid using a stud dog or brood bitch that could be described as 'nervy'. This behaviour can easily appear in the pups. It could be inherited; it could be learned in the nest from the mother – or both.

Research has shown that nervous mothers produce nervous puppies, even when the puppies have been fostered from another bitch. There is no certainty that the puppies will inherit a nervous temperament from their sire or dam, but it should give you cause to be cautious.

Aggression is a more difficult trait to categorise,

as it can be acquired in studs. Neil Ewart says: "I have known some studs dogs – and owned one – that loved a punch-up with another dog. However, it did not come out in any pups as the dog had learned this behaviour. Certainly, a generally sound temperament will normally come out in the offspring."

Good socialisation (see Chapter 7) will help even the most problematic puppy to overcome worries, but it must be remembered that you cannot alter the genetic make-up of the animal. A skilful owner can make improvements with training and socialisation, but the genetic weaknesses are actually being masked over and will remain. This does not mean that the pup will not develop into a perfectly acceptable adult, but there is no guarantee. It is very questionable whether such a dog should be considered for breeding, as the genes will not have altered.

If you meet a nervous dog, the owner will often state that the dog must have had a traumatic time earlier in life. This is often said of rescued dogs where the history is invariably unknown. However, Neil Ewart disputes the validity of these claims.

"I have judged the Best Condition Rescued Dog classes at shows on many occasions," he said. "In the process, I have handled a large number of dogs that have had the most horrendous experiences, including being set on fire. These dogs have

NEWBORN

- Puppies are born blind and deaf, with a weak sense of smell. They have no teeth, but a strong instinct to suck.
- A newborn pup can whine and yelp in pain, but cannot bark.
- The brain and the nervous system are immature – the twitching and stretching of limbs seen in very young puppies is a reflex action, which helps to develop the nervous system and the muscles.
- Puppies move around by slithering on their bellies. This takes a lot of effort so they rarely move from their mother's side.
- The puppy coat is soft. Texture and colour will often change as the pup matures.
- The puppies need the stimulus of the mother's licking in order to pass urine and faeces.

10-13 DAYS

- The puppies' eyes open. They are generally pale blue, but will darken over the next few weeks.
- It is believed that proper vision is not established until day 17.

2 WEEKS

- Hearing develops from two weeks of age.
- The ability to bark seems to coincide with the development of hearing.

2-3 WEEKS

- Milk teeth come through. Most breeders will introduce some solid food at this stage.
- The sense of smell becomes increasingly developed.

3 WEEKS

- The puppies will be on their feet, and becoming more active.
- They show an increasing desire to leave the nest and to follow their mother.
- The pups will now react to unexpected noises.
- All their senses are now fully developed, and they will be ready to explore their surroundings.

4 WEEKS

- Interaction between littermates becomes more frequent and intense, and a social hierarchy will develop within the litter.

5 WEEKS

- If the weather is fine, the puppies can be allowed outside in a puppy run for short periods.
  - They will show an interest in playing with toys and with each other.
- Maternal discipline will be given if games get too rough.

6-7 WEEKS

- Play-learning is a vital aspect of this period, and it is when most pups learn the basis of canine manners and communication.
  - Interaction with humans is very important, and as much time as possible should be given to handling and talking to the puppies.

generally been a pleasure to handle, and appear jolly and pleased to see everyone. It is quite obvious that, genetically, they are very sound for temperament, which has given them the capacity to overcome terrible trauma. This, coupled with the excellent work done by their new owners, is part of the jigsaw that, if all the parts come together, produces a sound and happy dog."

EARLY DAYS

There is nothing more appealing than seeing a contented litter of puppies with their mother. In the early days, it is often very hard to tell one puppy from another, but, in a matter of weeks, the puppies' individual personalities begin to emerge.

As the pups develop, the breeder's theories are put to the test. This is time to see whether the carefully planned litter has lived up to expectations.

THE GROWING PUPS

As a potential purchaser, you will have to wait until the pups are four to five weeks old before you are allowed to see them. However, it is interesting to chart a puppy's development so that you can imagine the world through their eyes.

The signs of good rearing – and good temperaments – are clear to see.

HANDLING

The puppies' development will be influenced by how much handling they receive in the first few weeks. The breeder should handle the puppies immediately after birth, and this should be stepped up as the puppies' senses develop and they become more responsive to outside stimuli. Mental and physical development is rapid, and the stimuli the puppies receive at this time will have a lasting effect on character and temperament.

The period between the third to the sixth week is most critical for the human-animal bond to become firmly established. The puppies should be encouraged to play, not only with each other but also with the breeder and other members of the family. If toys are provided, the pups will become more out-going and adventurous. As long as the weather is fine, the puppies will benefit from exploring the garden – provided they are closely supervised.

WHAT TO LOOK FOR

When you eventually track down a breeder who has puppies available, you will need to make an appointment to view the litter. If you are worried about making the right decision, do not hesitate to take someone along with you who does have

To begin with, it is hard to tell one puppy from another in the litter.

experience of puppies. After all, you would not buy a car without an 'expert' if your knowledge of mechanics was minimal.

BASIC REQUIREMENTS
Look for the following signs, which indicate that the puppies have been correctly reared:

- The living quarters should be clean and smell fresh.
- The puppies should be well covered but not fat. (A pot-bellied puppy may be infested with worms.)
- The puppies' coats should be clean, with no evidence of dirt, matting, or dandruff.
- The puppies' eyes should be bright, with no sign of discharge.
- Rear ends should be clean. A dirty behind could indicate the pup is suffering from diarrhoea.
- The pups should be lively and out-going.

HOME-REARING
Ideally, the puppies will have been reared in the breeder's home, and will have had all the benefits of early socialisation. They will have been handled by the breeder and their family, and will be accustomed to the sights and sounds of a busy household.

Guide Dogs has 250 brood bitches, and they all live with volunteer families. When a brood bitch is used for breeding, she stays with her family and has her litter at home. This has two big advantages. The brood bitch is more likely to be happy and relaxed to whelp and rear puppies in her own home, and the puppies get all the benefits of early socialisation. The puppies will hear the sounds of the washing machine, the vacuum cleaner, and all the other domestic appliances. They will hear the television, the radio, the doorbell, and all the different voices in the family. They will be handled on a regular basis,

and they will get used to the comings and goings of the family and occasional visitors.

In the past, nearly all the Guide Dog litters were whelped at the breeding centre, and so there has been the opportunity to compare the results of puppies bred in the two different environments. The results come out overwhelmingly in favour of home-bred litters. It has been found that puppies reared in kennels have a far higher level of distraction when they are being trained. This may take the form of a pup who has poor concentration and is easily distracted, or the pup may be particularly distracted by other dogs. The success rate of puppies reared at home and going on to qualify as guide dogs is significantly higher than among pups reared in kennels.

MATERNAL INFLUENCE
It is vital to see the puppies with their mother, as this will give you a very good indication of temperament. It is wise to favour a mum who appears kind and calm, and who shows few qualms

A brood bitch will be more relaxed if she has her puppies at home – and the pups benefit from lots of handling. This is brood bitch Imogen with her first litter.

Spend some time watching the puppies so that you can get an idea of individual personalities.

about strangers entering the house and handling her new babies. A mum that barks or growls could be teaching the pups that the human is a threat. It could also indicate a weak temperament, which she might have passed on to her pups.

During those early weeks in the nest, the mother has total influence over her puppies. The puppies watch how she behaves and how she reacts, and they take their lead from her. If she is out-going and friendly, this will help the puppies to grow in confidence. She is also the sole disciplinarian, and will give a warning growl if play gets too rough or if a pup steps out of line.

ASSESSING THE PUPPIES

What can you learn by looking at the puppies? First of all, you need the breeder to co-operate by letting you see the pups when they are most likely to be wide awake and lively. If the pups have been woken from a sleep and then fed, they will generally be at their most active. It is impossible to make a fair assessment of the pups if they are exhausted after a strenuous play session.

Hopefully, the pups will all run out to meet you, vying with each other to get attention. Beware of the puppy who hangs back and appears wary. You may think he looks sweet, but he is not showing the positive attitude that you are looking for. Some

pups appear more disinterested than others. This is not necessarily a drawback, as long as the pup is happy to come to you when approached and enjoys being fussed over.

Watch the puppies playing with each other – this will give you the best idea of their individual personalities, and of the hierarchy that has developed within the litter. Every litter has its different characters. There is the ringleader who is the first to investigate anything new, there is the clever pup who acts as the litter's problem-solver, there is the bossy pup who steals the toys from his siblings, and there is the laid-back individual who takes life in his stride.

As long as the puppies have the hallmarks of a good, sound temperament, showing a bold, out-going, and friendly attitude, you can simply look for the pup that appeals to you most. It is often said that puppies pick themselves, and there is certainly an element of truth in this. If you have an instinctive liking for a pup, it may well be because this is the type of pup that will suit you.

However, do listen to the breeder's advice, and be guided by their assessment of the puppies. A breeder will have spent many hours 'puppy watching' and is in a unique position to know the temperament of each member of the litter, to judge which particular pup is likely to fit in with your lifestyle.

TEMPERAMENT TESTING

A number of breeders carry out temperament tests so they can get a better idea of the individual puppies. This can be very useful in helping prospective buyers to pick puppies. For example, a puppy who clearly has a strong, dominant nature will need an owner who has some experience of training, whereas a quiet, calm puppy would be ideal for more elderly owners.

Guide Dogs carries out puppy aptitude tests when its puppies are around six weeks of age. It is at this point that the litter leaves the mother and comes into the breeding centre. The pups will stay in the centre for 36-48 hours before being placed with a puppy walker.

On arrival at the breeding centre, each pup will be given a thorough check, and will then be microchipped and vaccinated (see page 47). On the following day, when the pups have had a chance to settle, they will be tested.

It is important to bear in mind that puppy-testing is only one means of evaluating temperament. It needs to be combined with a sound knowledge of the breed's behavioural characteristics, and the breeder's observations.

TEST CONTROLS

The test should be carried out by a person who has spent little or no time with the pups previously and should, ideally, take place in an area that is unfamiliar to the pups. These two elements provide a way of checking each pup's reaction to a stranger and to a new environment. To help ensure accurate scoring, puppies should be awake before they are taken for testing, and testing should not take place shortly after pups have eaten. Where test results are unclear, testing can be repeated the next day. The testing area should be one that is removed from the litter area and with as few distractions as possible.

SOCIAL ATTRACTION

Place the puppy in the test area. From a few feet away, the tester coaxes the pup to him/her by clapping their hands gently and kneeling down. The tester must coax the pup in a direction away from the point where the puppy entered the testing area.

PURPOSE

Degree of social attraction, confidence or independence.

SCORE

1 = Came readily, tail up, jumped, bit at hands.
2 = Came readily, tail up, pawed, licked at hands.
3 = Came readily, tail up.
4 = Came readily, tail down.
5 = Came hesitantly, tail down.
6 = Did not come at all.

FOLLOWING

Stand up and walk away from the pup in a normal manner. Make sure the pup sees you walk away.

PURPOSE

Degree of following attraction. (Not following indicates independence.)

SCORE

1 = Followed readily, tail up, got underfoot, bit at feet.
2 = Followed readily, tail up, got underfoot.
3 = Followed readily, tail up.
4 = Followed readily, tail down.
5 = Followed hesitantly, tail down.
6 = Did not follow at all or moved away.

RESTRAINT

The tester holds the puppy on their lap, and gently rolls him on his back, holding him with one hand for a full 15 seconds.

PURPOSE

This measures the puppy's dominant or submissive tendency. It measures how the pup accepts stress when socially/physically dominated.

SCORE

1 = Struggled fiercely, flailed, bit.
2 = Struggled fiercely, flailed.
3 = Settled then struggled, then settled with some eye contact.
4 = Struggled then settled.
5 = No struggle.
6 = No struggle, straining to avoid eye contact.

SOCIAL DOMINANCE

Let the pup stand up, and gently stroke him from his head across the back while the tester crouches beside him. Continue stroking until a recognisable behaviour is established.

PURPOSE

Degree of acceptance of social dominance. The pup may try to dominate by jumping and nipping, or he may be independent and walk away.

SCORE

1 = Jumped, pawed, bit, growled.
2 = Jumped and pawed, or indifferent.
3 = Cuddles up to tester and tries to lick face.
4 = Squirmed, licked at hands.
5 = Rolled over, licked at hands.
6 = Went away and stayed away.

ELEVATION DOMINANCE

Bend over and cradle the pup under his belly, with your fingers interlaced and your palms turned up. Elevate the puppy just up from the ground, and hold him there for approximately 30 seconds.

PURPOSE

This measures the degree of accepting dominance while in a position of no control.

SCORE

1 = Struggled fiercely, bit, growled.
2 = Struggled fiercely.
3 = No struggle, relaxed.
4 = Struggled, then settled, licked.
5 = No struggle, licked at hands.
6 = No struggle, froze.

RETRIEVING

Crouch beside the pup and attract his attention with a crumpled-up paper ball or toy. When the pup shows interest and is watching, toss the object 4-6 feet in front of the pup.

PURPOSE

This measures the degree of willingness to work with a person. There is a high correlation between the ability to retrieve and successful guide dogs, obedience dogs and field trial dogs.

SCORE

1 = Chases object, picks up object and runs away.
2 = Chases object, stands over object, does not return.
3 = Chases object and returns with object to tester.
4 = Chases object and returns without object to tester.
5 = Starts to chase object, loses interest.
6 = Does not chase object.

SOUND SENSITIVITY

Place the pup in the centre of the testing area. The tester should make a noise a few feet away from the puppy (such as clapping hands, or dropping car keys or some other solid object).

PURPOSE

This measures sensitivity to sound.

SCORE

1 = Listens, locates sound, walks towards it barking.
2 = Listens, locates sound, barks.
3 = Listens, locates sound, shows curiosity and walks towards sound.
4 = Listens and locates the sound.
5 = Cringes, backs off, hides.
6 = Ignores sound, shows no curiosity.

SIGHT SENSITIVITY

Place the pup in the centre of the area. Tie a string around a large towel and jerk it across the floor a few feet away from the puppy.

PURPOSE

This measures the degree of intelligent response to a strange object.

SCORE

1 = Looks, attacks and bites.
2 = Looks, barks, tail up.
3 = Looks curiously, attempts to investigate.
4 = Looks, barks, tail-tuck.
5 = Runs away, hides.
6 = Ignores, shows no curiosity.

SCORING

Overall scoring is achieved by averaging out the scores given for all tests i.e. totalling up the points scored and dividing by the eight exercises.

THE R LITTER

At Guide Dogs, all members of a litter have names beginning with the same initial, which aids record-keeping and identification. In the following 'R' litter, eight German Shepherd puppies bred by Guide Dogs were tested. If a litter is carefully planned, you would expect scoring to be fairly consistent between members of the litter.

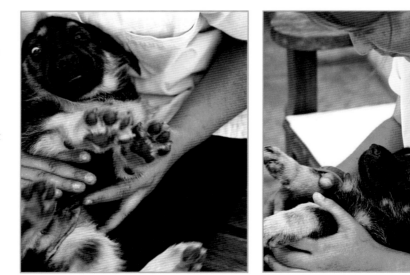

The Restraint exercise provided some contrasts, varying from a couple of pups who struggled (pictured left) to the pups who put up no resistance (right).

THE R LITTER – TEMPERAMENT TESTING RESULTS

Puppy Name	Ruby	Roddy	Rebecca	Rudolph	Rebel	Robbie	Roscoe	Ronan
Date of Birth	01.06.03	01.06.03	01.06.03	01.06.03	01.06.03	01.06.03	01.06.03	01.06.03
Dog/Bitch	B	D	B	D	D	D	D	D
Sire	Samson	Samson	Samson	Samson	Samson	Samson	Samson	Samson
Dam	Trudy	Trudy	Trudy	Trudy	Trudy	Trudy	Trudy	Trudy
Social Attraction	3	3	2	2	2	2	3	3
Following	2	2	2	2	2	2	2	3
Restraint	2	2	2	2	2	3	5	5
Social Dominance	3	3	3	3	3	3	3	3
Elevation Dominance	3	3	3	3	3	3	2	3
Retrieving	4	3	6	4	4	4	3	6
Sound Sensitivity	3	3	6	3	3	6	3	4
Sight Sensitivity	3	3	3	3	3	3	3	4
Dominance Average	2.666666667	2.666666667	2.666666667	2.666666667	2.666666667	3	3.333333333	3.666666667
Willingness Average	2.5	2.5	2	2	2	2	2.5	3
Distraction Average	4	3	6	4	4	4	3	6
Suspicion Average	3	3	4.5	3	3	4.5	3	4
Total Score	23	22	27	22	22	26	24	31
Average Score	2.875	2.75	3.375	2.75	2.75	3.25	3	3.875
Grade	2	2	3	2	2	3	3	3
Average Litter Score	3.078125	3.078125	3.078125	3.078125	3.078125	3.078125	2.078125	3.078125
Average Litter Grade	3	3	3	3	3	3	3	3
Comments								Not as confident as littermates.

Most of the pups showed an interest in the retrieve object. A couple of pups proved to be born retrievers (above), while two others showed no desire to chase (right).

Most pups had a similar response to Sound Sensitivity, but a couple of pups ignored the sound completely.

Only one pup scored a 4 in the Sight Sensitivity test, looking at the object and barking with tail tucked.

INTERPRETING THE SCORES

The test is based on a series of puppy tests developed by William E. Campbell

A   1-1.9   An extremely dominant puppy who may be aggressive and who can easily be provoked to bite. The pup's dominant nature will cause him to resist human leadership, demanding an experienced and capable handler. This type of puppy should not be selected for guide dog work.

B   2-2.9   Dominant and self-assured. The pup can be provoked to bite; however, he readily accepts human leadership that is firm, consistent and knowledgeable. This is not an ideal pup for guide dog work or for a tentative, indecisive handler. In the right hands, this type has the potential to become a good dog, provided the owners know what they are doing.

C   3-3.9   This pup is out-going and friendly, and will adjust well in situations in which he receives regular training and exercise. He has a flexible temperament that adapts well to different types of environment, provided he is handled correctly. A good guide dog type.

WHAT CAN BE GAINED?

In Guide Dog litters, all the puppies are placed with puppy walkers unless there is an outstanding health problem. So, for the present, the aptitude tests are not used in terms of selecting or rejecting puppies for training.

Simon Blythe, Head of Genetics and Reproduction at Guide Dogs, says: "At the moment, we are using the tests as one of the many elements in building up a complete picture of a puppy from birth, progressing through puppy walking, and how he responds to advanced training. We need to wait until the puppies have completed this cycle before we can assess the significance of the aptitude tests. They could become relevant in selecting the most suitable puppies for guide dog work, or they could help us to identify areas where a puppy needs specific help and support during puppy walking."

The T litter comprised of five dogs and three bitches.

THE T LITTER

Guide Dogs has a remarkable record of success in breeding puppies that go on to qualify, and, every so often, it hits the jackpot and everything goes right.

This happened with the T litter, which was sired by stud dog Ufton, a Golden Retriever, out of brood bitch Yuma, a Labrador Retriever. Eight

D	**4-4.9**	An easily controlled, adaptable puppy whose submissive nature will make him continually look to his master for leadership. This pup is easy to train, reliable with children, and though possibly lacking some self-confidence, should make a reasonable guide dog or a high-quality family pet. Less out-going than a pup scoring in the 3s, but his demeanour is gentle and affectionate.
E	**5-5.9**	An extremely submissive pup, lacking in self-confidence. This type of pup will bond very closely with his owner and requires regular companionship and encouragement to bring him out of himself. If handled incorrectly, this pup will grow up to be very shy and fearful. For this reason, not an ideal guide dog type.
F	**6-6.9**	A puppy that scores 6 consistently is uninterested in people. He will mature into a dog who is not demonstrably affectionate and who has a low need for human company. In general, it is rare to see properly socialised pups test in this way; however, breeds that have been bred for specific tasks (e.g. Foxhounds and Malamutes) can exhibit this level of independence. To perform as intended, these dogs require a singularity of purpose uncompromised by strong attachments to the owner. Not suitable for guide dog work.

Brood bitch Yuma.

Stud dog Ufton.

puppies were born in the litter: five dogs (Toffee, Tom, Tucker, Tony and Tyler) and three bitches (Trusty, Tweedie and Tumble) – and they all qualified as guide dogs.

STUD DOG UFTON
Ufton comes from a very strong line. His father, Guidewell Gunner, has proved particularly successful as a stud dog.

RECORD TO DATE
Sired 220 pups
94 have, so far, qualified as guide dogs
16 rejected from training
1 has been kept as a brood
109 are still being trained or puppy walked for Guide Dogs.

BROOD BITCH YUMA
Yuma is from a very good and proven line for guide dogs. Her grandfather was a very successful stud. Her dam line goes back to the famous Sandylands stud dog, Sh. Ch. Sandylands Myrainbeau.

RECORD TO DATE
Produced 28 pups
18 have qualified
1 kept as a brood
4 are either being trained or puppy walked
5 rejected (1 as a result of an accident).

LEAVING HOME
The eight puppies were placed with puppy walkers, supervised by schemes in different parts of the country.

PUPPY	DESTINATION
Toffee	Leamington
Trusty	Leamington
Tweedie	Bolton

Tom	Bolton
Tumble	Wokingham
Tucker	Wokingham
Tony	Wokingham
Tyler	Tollgate

The advantage of distributing a litter in different regions is that the puppies will come under the care of a number of different supervisors. This means that a more objective assessment can be made of the litter as a whole, rather than relying on one person's assessment.

All puppies have their own computer number, and monthly reports on the puppies are logged into the system. This gives a complete profile of the litter, and it also means that supervisors can match the progress of the puppies in their care against the other members of the litter. This can be very useful if problems arise, as the supervisor can see if the problem is common to the litter, or if it is something that has arisen during training and socialisation.

THE T LITTER IN TRAINING

The eight pups were all accepted for training as guide dogs. Their trainers had the following comments to make when they were ready to be matched to guide dog owners:

Tucker: Minimal distractions combined with good progress. Good, relaxed approach to work, which is consistent.

Tyler: Sensitive dog but has made good progress throughout training.

Tweedie: Generally positive and willing working on known routes.

Tumble: A responsive and generally easily handled type with excellent social behaviour.

Toffee: Very good progress. Has settled into a routine and is able to cope with a variety of conditions.

Tom: Responds to everything asked of him, and is a nice type with good potential.

Tony: A willing and responsive dog. Confident and consistent.

Trust: A bright, easily controlled bitch with no vices.

REPEAT MATING

The all-star litter produced by Ufton and Yuma was a result of the good, strong lines in both the sire and the dam, and the use of first crosses of the Labrador and Golden Retriever.

A mating such as this breeds out some of the boisterous nature of the Labrador, and some of the sensitivity of the Golden Retriever.

Because of the success of the T litter, Guide Dogs has recently repeated the same mating. There is obviously no guarantee that it will be as good, but the chances of producing some quality puppies are high.

This will be Yuma's last litter as all broods are retired by eight years of age.

STRIKING A DEAL

While you are assessing the breeder and their methods of rearing, the breeder will also be assessing you. Do not be surprised if you get third-degree questioning before you are allowed to buy a pup. A responsible breeder will want to establish whether you can provide a suitable home for a dog before agreeing to sell.

If both parties are happy and you decide to buy a puppy, you will probably be asked to pay a deposit to reserve your pup. If there are similar puppies in the litters – such as a litter of black Labradors – the breeder will mark your pup (usually with a dab of nail varnish on some part of his body) to distinguish him from his littermates. This will quickly disappear after your pup has arrived in his new home.

When you collect your pup, there will be some paperwork to sort out, as well as paying for the pup in full (see page 52).

THE ALL-STAR T LITTER

Tony based in Southend on Sea.

Tom based in Tyne and Wear.

Tyler based in Lancashire.

Toffee.

Tucker
based in
Hampshire.

Trumble
based in
Buckingham-
shire.

Trusty.

Tweedie
based in
Tyne and
Wear.

CHAPTER FOUR

THE HOMECOMING

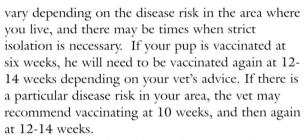

O nce you have chosen your puppy, make every endeavour to get him home between six and eight weeks of age. This may sound too young, but these really are the formative weeks of his life for temperament. A pup will be very responsive to his new human family, and will be ready to make a strong and lasting bond. The mothers do not miss their offspring at this age. In fact, they are usually heartily relieved to have their freedom again.

VACCINATION POLICY

If you can get your pup at the recommended age, the risk of the puppy contracting an infectious disease is minimal if you follow certain safeguards. The mother must be fully inoculated, and you must find out if your vet is happy to give the pup his first vaccination as soon as he arrives in his new home.

Experience in the Guide Dogs' kennels, stretching over 30 years, shows that puppies respond to the vaccination at six weeks. This allows the puppy enough protection to be taken out of the strict isolation that was once thought to be essential. This is of enormous benefit, as it is now widely recognised that the sooner a pup is exposed to the sights and sounds of the outside world, the better it will be for his development (see Chapter 7).

Most veterinary surgeons are willing to use a vaccine at six weeks, but it is best to discuss vaccination policy before visiting the surgery with your new puppy. The timing of vaccinations may

vary depending on the disease risk in the area where you live, and there may be times when strict isolation is necessary. If your pup is vaccinated at six weeks, he will need to be vaccinated again at 12-14 weeks depending on your vet's advice. If there is a particular disease risk in your area, the vet may recommend vaccinating at 10 weeks, and then again at 12-14 weeks.

There are some breeders, and some veterinary surgeons, who emphasise the risk of a puppy going outside the home before he is fully protected.

All Guide Dog puppies are vaccinated at six weeks.

However, this may mean waiting until the pup is 15 weeks old, which would be most detrimental to his socialisation.

There are some places that should be avoided, even if the pup has been vaccinated at six weeks. Do not take your pup to heavily used public parks or grass verges, or let him sniff around lampposts. Common sense will tell you to steer well clear of anywhere that is regularly frequented by other dogs.

GETTING READY

In most cases, you will have a week or two to wait before your pup is ready to come home. This time can be well spent buying the equipment you need, and preparing your house and garden for your new arrival.

BUYING EQUIPMENT

You can spend as much or as little as you like buying a host of dog accessories, but, in fact, a puppy has only a few basic requirements.

BED AND BEDDING

Every dog needs a place to call his own, and this usually takes the form of a bed or an indoor kennel (see below). This is somewhere the dog can rest undisturbed, and where he will sleep at night.

You can start off by customising a cardboard box:
- Remove metal staples.
- Take off the flaps.
- Cut down the front so your pup can get in and out.
- Line with soft bedding.

This will give your pup a cosy home, which you can discard as soon as it is outgrown, or replace if it gets chewed.

The best type of permanent accommodation is a plastic kidney-shaped dog bed. These come in a wide range of sizes, so make sure you buy one that will be big enough for your pup when he is fully-grown. When it is lined with bedding, this makes a comfortable bed, which is easy to clean and is virtually indestructible.

You can use an old blanket for bedding, but the synthetic fleece bedding, made specially for dogs, is much more user-friendly. It is made so that moisture soaks straight through it, which can be useful when your puppy is still learning to be clean at night. The bedding is machine-washable and dries quickly. The best plan is to buy two pieces of bedding: one to use, and one as a spare. You may find it useful to buy an additional piece of bedding to use in the car (see page 102)

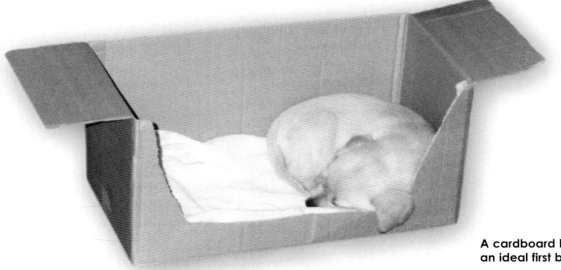

A cardboard box makes an ideal first bed.

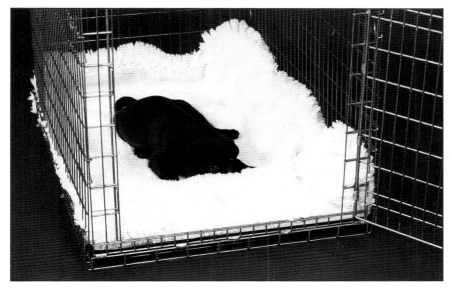

An indoor kennel will prove to be an invaluable investment.

INDOOR KENNELS

An indoor kennel is the most expensive item to buy, but most dog owners would argue that it is an invaluable investment. Many Guide Dog puppy walkers, who take on a new puppy year after year, cannot imagine rearing a pup without one.

An indoor kennel is useful in the following ways:

- It provides a safe, secure place for the pup when he cannot be supervised.
- The puppy can sleep in his indoor kennel overnight, and you can be confident that he cannot get up to any mischief.
- If you already have a dog, the indoor kennel provides a safe place for the pup at night, and at times when you are not around to supervise the two animals (see page 55).
- Using an indoor kennel can speed up the process of house-training (see page 62).
- A pup who is accustomed to an indoor kennel is happy to spend short periods on his own, and this prevents separation anxiety problems from developing (see page 123).
- An indoor kennel can be used in the car, providing a safe way to travel (see page 102).
- An indoor kennel can be used if you are staying away from home, where it literally becomes a 'home from home' for your pup.

It is important to train your pup to go into his indoor kennel so that he learns to regard it as his own safe haven (see page 62).

STAIR-GATE

This is useful if you want to prevent your puppy going upstairs. It can also be used as a barrier between rooms if you want to confine your pup to specific areas of the house.

BOWLS

You will need two bowls: one for food and one for water. There are plenty of different types available, but, in terms of durability and hygiene, stainless steel bowls are a sensible choice.

FOOD

It is important to continue with the type of food your puppy is used to, at least to begin with (see page 61). A sudden change could lead to a stomach upset. The breeder may provide you with enough food for the first few meals, but it is a good idea to find out the diet that is being fed, and get a supply.

COLLAR AND LEAD

Buy a lightweight collar, which will not be too cumbersome for your puppy to wear. Your pup's

WHAT'S IN A NAME?

It is important to decide on your pup's name before he arrives home. If you wait to see what suits your pup, you will end up with a very confused animal. Ideally, choose a name that is one or two syllables in length, which will be easier for both you and your pup.

neck size will keep changing as he grows, so try to get an adjustable collar, which will last him for the first few months.

For initial training, the lead you buy should also be reasonably lightweight (bearing in mind the size of your puppy). Make sure it has a secure trigger fastening.

ID

Your puppy will need some form of identity. This can be a disc, engraved with your contact details. You might want consider a permanent form of ID, such as having your pup microchipped. This is a simple procedure, which can be carried out by your vet.

GROOMING GEAR

This will depend on the breed you have chosen, and it is best to seek advice from the puppy's breeder. Regardless of breed, it is important to accustom your pup to being groomed and handled right from the start. A soft brush is useful for this aspect of your pup's education.

Regular teeth-cleaning and nail-clipping will also be part of routine care, and a pup who is accustomed to this from an early age will be quite happy to accept the attention. You can buy a toothbrush or a finger brush, and there are special meaty-flavour toothpastes made especially for dogs.

You can use a file to keep nails in trim, or you may prefer to use guillotine-type nail-clippers. It is important to trim only the tip of the nail so you do not cut the quick, which will bleed profusely. It is a good idea to ask your vet, or a veterinary nurse at the practice, to help you with this procedure until you feel confident.

For advice on grooming, see page 77.

TOYS

When it comes to choosing toys, you will be spoilt for choice. There are numerous dog toys available,

Make sure the toys you buy are 100 per cent safe.

and you can build up a collection over the years to come. Make sure the toys you choose are 100 per cent safe, as even a young puppy can chew his way through plastic. Squeaker toys are fun, but play sessions should always be supervised as a pup can rip through the toy and then swallow the squeaker. Hard rubber toys are puppy safe, as are cotton tug toys.

Remember that your pup may 'outgrow' his toys. A small toy that was safe for a puppy to play with may become hazardous as your pup gets bigger.

You can save money by providing your pup with a plastic bottle, ensuring that you have removed the cap and all parts of the seal. This cheap but effective toy is recommended to all Guide Dog puppy walkers, and they report that it is rated a firm favourite!

Toys are very much dual-purpose – they are fun for your puppy, and they are an excellent training aid (see page 72).

CLEAN UP!

Cleaning up after your pup is not one of the most attractive aspects of owning a dog, but it is essential to be prepared on all occasions when you take your puppy out in public places.

You can buy plastic bags or a 'pooper-scooper', depending on which you find easier to use, or you can simply re-use supermarket plastic bags or similar.

SLEEPING QUARTERS

You will need to decide where to locate your puppy's bed/indoor kennel before he arrives. From your pup's point of view, it should be somewhere that is free from draughts; it should be warm in the winter and relatively cool in the summer. Most owners find the kitchen or the utility room the most convenient place to choose.

If you want your pup to be with you in the sitting room, or elsewhere, you can buy a second bed, which he can use as temporary quarters.

An inquisitive pup can always find trouble...

PUPPY-PROOFING YOUR HOME

One good thing about having a puppy in your home is that it teaches you to be tidy! If you leave your best shoes lying about and your puppy chews them, there is only one person to blame.

There are a number of household hazards that you should watch out for:

- Tidy up trailing electrical wires so that they are out of reach.
- Keep household cleaning products (e.g. bleach and disinfectant) in a secure cupboard.
- If you are feeding a complete dried diet, make sure it is stored in a cupboard that your puppy cannot possibly penetrate.
- A trailing tablecloth could easily be tugged by an inquisitive pup – and the results could be disastrous.
- Potted plants may not survive for long if your pup can reach them – and there is a danger that some plants may be poisonous to dogs (see page 52).

Look at your house from your puppy's perspective, and try to work out the best way to guard your valuables and to keep your puppy safe.

IN THE GARDEN

When your pup first arrives home, he will be only too keen to stick by you. But as he grows bolder, he may decide to make a bid for freedom.

- Make sure all fencing is secure, and that it is a suitable height for the breed you are buying.
- If you have a gate, check that the catch is secure, and remind everyone in the family to be meticulous about keeping it closed.
- Garden ponds are a source of irresistible attraction to puppies, so it is a good idea to construct some type of covering to prevent unscheduled pond-dipping.
- If you have a garden shed, make sure it is securely fastened, particularly if you are storing chemicals such as pesticides.
- Bin-raiding can be tempting, so if your dustbins are in the garden, make sure the lids are secured.

It is a good idea to select a specific toilet area in the garden for your puppy. This makes cleaning up easier, and, more importantly, your pup will learn that this is the place where he goes to relieve himself.

POISONOUS PLANTS

There are a number of garden plants that are poisonous to dogs, and so it is worth checking the list below to prevent a potentially serious situation arising. Eating poisonous plants can cause sickness, diarrhoea, and in extreme cases, paralysis, coma, and even death.

- Amarylis
- Azalea
- Cyclamen
- Daffodil bulbs
- Dumb cane *dieffenbachia*
- Elderberry
- English ivy
- Foxglove
- Holly berries
- Hyacinth
- Iris
- Laurel
- Lily of the Valley
- Milkweed
- Mistletoe
- Nightshade
- Oleander
- Philodendron
- Poinsettia
- Primrose
- Privet
- Ragwort
- Rhododendron
- Spider plant
- Stinging nettle
- Wisteria
- Yew

COLLECTING YOUR PUPPY

At last, it is time to collect your puppy. If possible, take a 'helper' with you, who will be able to look after the puppy while you drive the car. The best plan is to collect your pup as early in the day as possible so that he has the maximum amount of time to settle in his new home before nightfall.

As well as paying the outstanding sum for your puppy, there will be some paperwork to sort out with the breeder. You should be provided with the following:

- A pedigree. This is your puppy's family tree, showing his family on his sire and his dam's side. It may go back three or sometimes five generations. It is customary for Champions in the family to be underlined in red.
- Details of Kennel Club registration, and a form for transfer of ownership.
- A diet sheet. This should state the type of food, the quantity currently being fed, and the number of meals per day. Many breeders will make up a diet sheet to extend over the first 12 months, which will guide you through from puppyhood to adulthood.
- Sample of diet. Some breeders provide enough food to cover the first few meals.
- Worming programme. This should include details of worming treatments carried out, and when the next treatment is due.
- Contact details so that you can seek the breeder's advice at any stage after you have bought your puppy.

ARRIVING HOME

It is a bewildering experience for a puppy to be separated from his mother and littermates, and to arrive in a completely new environment. Some pups stride in as if they own the place, others are more sensitive and need lots of reassurance.

Do not make the mistake of inviting friends and neighbours to inspect the new arrival. Your puppy will have his work cut out meeting his new family and familiarising himself with his new home.

Start by taking your pup to his toilet area in the

Arriving in a new home is a bewildering experience for a puppy.

garden. He will probably relieve himself within a couple of minutes, so give plenty of praise. (For more information on house-training, see page 62.) Allow the pup to explore the garden, but stay with him to supervise, and to give him a chance to get used to your voice and smell.

Then take your pup into the house, and show him his sleeping quarters. Let him investigate, giving lots of verbal encouragement to boost his confidence.

MEETING THE FAMILY

Let the puppy meet each member of the family in turn. It helps if you have some treats, and then your pup can be called and given a treat. Let each person stroke the pup, and let the pup have a good sniff so that he learns who belongs to his new family.

If you have children, try to keep introductions calm, so that no one gets over-excited. Young children should sit on the floor to be introduced to the puppy, to avoid any danger of the pup being dropped. After giving a treat, and making sure the puppy takes it gently, you can introduce a toy. Play sessions should always be supervised, especially with children of toddler age. Your job is to make sure the children are not too rough and the puppy does not get too hyped up.

GOLDEN RULES

Children and dogs can have a most rewarding relationship, but first a sense of mutual respect must be established. If you stick to the following guidelines, your puppy should soon be fully integrated with the younger members of the family.

- Teach children not to manhandle the pup. He should be stroked, but he should not have his ears yanked or his tail pulled.
- When the puppy is sleeping, or eating his food, he should not be disturbed.
- Do not allow the puppy to jump up at the children, or to chase after them when they are running.
- Discourage your puppy from mouthing and play-biting (see page 77).

Puppies and children can become the best of friends.

53

Alison Malcolm is the mother of four children: Giles (5), Phoebe (7), Izzie (13) and Ellie (16). As the children have been growing up, she has walked four Guide Dog puppies, and has recently taken charge of Quip, a Flat coat-Golden Retriever cross.

"Quip is the most laid-back puppy I have ever had," said Alison. "He has settled in with us as if he has always lived here."

When Alison takes her two youngest children to school, Quip always comes too.

"Quip gets swamped by all the children who want to stroke him. I always encourage them to stroke Quip on his head rather than trying to touch him all over, and I always explain that he's just a baby, and he won't do any harm. It's a sad fact that some children are frightened of dogs – even small puppies. I think they get it from their parents, and no one tells them how to behave around dogs."

AT SCHOOL

As a special guide dog puppy, Quip is allowed to go into school, and he goes round the classrooms saying hello to everyone.

"He's a real celebrity," said Alison. "I then take him home via the local shops, and so he has an excellent spell of socialisation to start the day."

At home, Alison imposes a number of doggy rules.

"We have an adult dog, a Weimaraner called Fitz, and so my children are used to being with dogs, but they often have friends come to play, and so it is important to have certain rules.

"Jumping up, and chasing small children can develop into a problem if you do not stop it right from the start. I tell the children to stop running, stand still, and then turn to face the pup, crouching down to his level.

"In this way, the pup has lost the motive to chase or jump up, and if the child is facing the pup on his level, they are in control."

PUPPY TOYS

Toys can be contentious, so Alison takes her children out to buy toys for the puppy.

"The children know where the toys are kept and they usually have one that they especially like. If the pup gets hold of one of their toys, they know to swap it with one of his toys. They also give him a toy if he tries to mouth them.

"The only other important rule is that the children must never disturb the puppy when he is sleeping. Puppies are like babies, and they really do need a lot of sleep. It is great to have a play session, but then the pup must be allowed to rest in peace."

Top dog: Quip with Giles and Phoebe.

- Supervise play sessions, and do not allow games of tug to develop. The puppy must always 'give up' the toy at the end of a game.
- Monitor noise levels, and stop children from shouting and screaming. It may be only in play, but it sends confusing messages to a young puppy.
- Try to ensure that children's toys are kept out of puppy's reach. This will prevent toys from being chewed, and will avoid the risk of the puppy swallowing potentially hazardous objects.

THE RESIDENT DOG

If you already have a dog at home, you will need to introduce the puppy. The best place to choose for the meeting is the garden, as the resident dog will not feel so territorial when he is outside.

Put the older dog on the lead, and allow the puppy to approach. In most cases, the pup will submit to the older dog, crouching low on the ground, and sometimes rolling on to his back. The pup may then try to instigate a game. Some adult dogs take to puppies straightaway. They do not feel threatened and are ready to welcome the new arrival. Other dogs are a little more suspicious, and may give a warning growl if the pup is pushing his luck.

As long as you are confident that the adult is not showing undue aggression, you should allow the two animals to sort themselves out. Let the adult off the lead, and allow both dogs to sniff each other. Do not reprimand the adult if he tells off the puppy. The pup has to learn to respect the older dog's authority, and a couple of warnings are usually sufficient for the boldest puppy. Within a couple of days, or even less, the two dogs will have established their relationship with each other, and, in most cases, they will enjoy each other's company.

It is a good idea to use an indoor kennel for your puppy at night if the two dogs are to sleep in the same room, or at any other time when you cannot supervise them. If the two dogs have been introduced properly, it is unlikely that trouble will suddenly arise – but it is always better to be safe than sorry.

Remember not to neglect your adult dog in all the excitement of having a new puppy at home.

Play sessions should always be supervised.

Make sure the adult has some quality time alone with you. This is easy to arrange as the pup will be too young to go for walks, and so you can ensure that these outings become a highspot for the older dog.

Equally, you will need to ensure that the puppy does not get too focused on his canine chum and become too dog-orientated. Allow time to train the puppy away from the older dog, and, when you start socialising your puppy (see Chapter 7), he should be taken out on his own, as well as with the resident dog. For more information on canine relations, see page 115.

Carol Evans is one of Guide Dogs' most dedicated volunteers. She has been a puppy walker for 22 years, and, during that time, she has also looked after guide dog brood bitches and has bred 22 litters to date. Ruby, the first puppy she walked, went on to become a brood bitch, and she was the start of a dynasty of guide dogs that have been bred by Carol. She now has three generations of Labrador guide dog brood bitches living at home: Ruby's daughter Jonie, now aged 15, her daughter Callie, aged 9, and her daughter Imogen, who is two-and-a-half.

In addition, Carol has a retired German Shepherd brood bitch, and she nearly always has a guide dog puppy going through its training.

"I keep saying I'm going to give up puppy walking but I'm a bit like a drug addict – it's easier to keep going than to give up," says Carol.

Carol has walked puppies from her own brood bitches, but she admits that she likes the challenge of walking puppies from other lines.

"It is rewarding to walk a puppy that you have bred, but I think you know them almost too well. You know everything about them. A homebred puppy just slots in so that you hardly know you've got a pup at all."

Carol's brood bitches have been very successful over the years, and the breeding line is highly valued by Guide Dogs.

SENSITIVE SIDE

"The puppies I have bred tend to be on the sensitive side," she says. "They are not so much the typical, brash Labrador, they tend to be more responsive. The feedback I have had from trainers and from guide dog owners is that they are very much 'people' dogs. Although they are sensitive, they are easy to handle and won't stand for being pushed around.

Sometimes a dog has proved to be a little too sensitive for guide dog work. One dog was worried about working in harness, but her extra sensitivity was put to good use. She was retrained and is now working as a dog for the disabled."

Carol has puppy walked a variety of breeds,

Four generations of guide dog breeding (pictured left to right): Grandmother Josie, aged 15, grand-daughter Imogen with her first litter of pups, and Imogen's mother Callie, aged nine.

Puppies will always take liberties, but adults are surprisingly tolerant.

including Labradors, Labrador-Retriever crosses, Golden Retrievers, Curly Coat Retriever crosses, and German Shepherds.

TRANSITIONS

"All the puppies have had their own personalities," she says. "But the German Shepherds do get under your skin. When a Labrador goes into training, you know he'll be fine as long as there's food on the table, but the Shepherds become so attached you worry they are never going to cope on their own. They do find the transitions between puppy walker and trainer, and then trainer and guide dog owner difficult, but those that can cope with the stress make wonderful working dogs."

Carol is used to puppies coming and going, and so are her resident brood bitches.

"If I puppy walk one of the puppies I have bred, they scarcely notice that we have an extra puppy in the family. But if a pup comes in from outside, I always supervise introductions. The two younger bitches, Callie and Imogen, are very puppy orientated, and they accept a new pup very quickly. But Jonie, my oldest Labrador, has a short fuse if she is pestered. She will give a warning growl if the pup pushes her too far, and I think that is a good thing. It is natural for an older dog to put a puppy in its place, and, as long as the situation

does not get out of hand, you should allow the dogs to sort things out."

Carol does not believe in taking chances; if she goes out, she always leaves the puppy in an indoor kennel.

"It is more a matter of being safe rather than sorry," she says. "I can't imagine anything happening, but it is better to be absolutely certain. I sometimes board a puppy for a few nights if the puppy walker is away on holiday, and so it pays to be extra careful."

At present, Carol is puppy walking Cinders, a Curly Coat-Labrador cross, and, despite her years of experience, Carol is finding her quite a handful.

CHALLENGE

"I say I like a challenge, and I've certainly got one this time! Cinders is a lovely dog, and she works brilliantly. But she gets really hyped up – she's on the go all the time – so I am keeping her a couple of months longer than usual, to give her a chance to mature and settle down."

With the brood bitches, the puppies she breeds, and the puppies she walks, life is hectic, but for Carol, it is hugely rewarding.

"Of course it's hard work, but the dogs are an absolute joy. I just feel so lucky to have had so many wonderful dogs sharing my life."

Relationships between dogs and cats can blossom – but take care in the early stages.

FELINE RELATIONS

Dogs and cats can become the best of friends, but this is definitely a relationship that has to be worked at. In fact, a puppy and a kitten that are brought up together will have few misunderstandings, and will grow up to live in perfect harmony – sometimes even sharing a bed.

However, the more likely scenario is introducing a puppy to an adult cat. If you already have a dog, your cat will have learnt essential rules, such as not running when the dog is about, and introductions will be much easier. But if your cat is not used to dogs, let alone a bouncy puppy, you will need to exercise a little tact.

- If you use an indoor kennel, start by confining your pup and allowing the cat to investigate.
- The next step is to hold your puppy and let the cat come into the same room. Have some treats at the ready, and if your pup gets too focused on the cat, divert his attention by giving him a treat.
- Keep repeating this routine over a period of days, rewarding your pup when he responds to you rather than the cat.

- Now try without restraining the puppy. You can coincide this with your puppy's mealtime. He will be so interested in eating his food that he will scarcely notice the cat.
- Work on this for a few days, and you will find that the novelty wears off for both puppy and cat. Make sure you supervise all interactions, and check that the door is left open or there is somewhere out of reach where the cat can escape if the pup is too boisterous.

MY FAMILY AND OTHER ANIMALS

A puppy must learn to live in harmony with members of his new family, and that might include rabbits, guinea pigs, or other small, furry animals. In some cases, the extended family may include a bird in a cage or chickens in a run.

Whatever animal you keep, the pup must learn to be accepting and tolerant. He must understand that the rabbit, for example, is not *his* to chase and harass. It is *your* rabbit, and therefore it is off-limits.

- Introduce the puppy to your pet, making sure it is securely confined in its hutch or its cage. When the pup shows an interest, divert his attention by giving a treat.

Socialisation can breed remarkable tolerance.

Kathy Williams is a new puppy walker for Guide Dogs, and Nancy, a black Labrador, is settling in well to her new home – although she has discovered that the house really belongs to Bramble, a ginger and white cat.

"Bramble is the boss, there's no doubt about that," said Kathy. "He accepts any dogs in our house, but he is in charge."

Bramble was bought up with Kathy's two Collies, Judy and Hop-A-Long, who lived until they were 17 and 19 respectively.

"Bramble liked to sleep between the two dogs, and if they didn't make enough room, he would sleep on top of them.

Bramble has already taught Nancy 'cat manners'.

TREAT TIME

"We used to give the Collies a treat in the evening, and they would have to sit first. Bramble would always come up to join us, and when we said: 'Sit', he would get his treat!"

Kathy now has a two-year-old Collie called Minstrel as well as her guide dog puppy, Nancy.

"Bramble accepted Nancy without turning a hair," said Kathy. "In fact, our puppy walking supervisor bought Nancy's sister, Nessie, to our house, and Bramble took one look as if to say: 'Not another one!' "

CAT CHASING

The big advantage of having a cat that has been brought up with dogs is that the cat does not run at the sight of a dog. If the cat doesn't run, the dog has nothing to chase, and so the idea of cat chasing never occurs.

"Nancy has never tried to chase Bramble. If she gets a bit too rough with him, he will put up a paw as if to say: 'Stop', but he always keeps his claws in."

Bramble is often the one who wants to play, and he pads at Nancy with his paw, trying to start a game.

"Obviously we are careful with Nancy's eyes, which are vulnerable, but I don't think Bramble would ever scratch. He really is a laid-back cat. To be honest, I really think that Bramble considers himself a dog!"

As a kitten, Bramble was quick to take control.

JUST LOOKING

Puppywalker Carol Evans has a readymade opportunity for socialising the puppies in her care with small animals. She keeps rabbits and guinea pigs in a hutch in the garden.

"The puppies I have bred here don't take any notice, but if I have a new pup or a temporary boarder, they can get a bit fixated until the novelty wears off. Guinea pigs are such shy creatures that they will run for cover if a pup comes rushing up. As far as the pup is concerned, that has the makings of a good game.

"To start with, I take the pup to the hutch and let him have a look. I correct any unruly behaviour, and, if the pup looks away, I really praise him. I keep repeating this until the pup learns how to behave. The Labradors usually lose interest quite quickly, but the Shepherd has a stronger chase instinct and they can take a little longer."

- If your pup is excited by what he sees and tries to get too close, say "No" or "Leave", and use a treat to get the puppy's attention focused on you.
- Repeat this over a period of days, making sure you reward your pup when he responds to you. Any attempt to get too close should be met with a growled "No" or "Leave" so that the pup understands that this is undesirable behaviour.

In most cases, the pup will soon lose interest in the cage or the hutch, but make sure the puppy is never left unsupervised in the presence of caged animals. A growing pup can forget his manners if he suddenly becomes excited.

There are wonderful stories of the most unlikely friendships developing between dogs and small pets, but a youngster cannot be relied upon.

MEALTIMES

Your puppy will probably be accustomed to four meals a day, so after he has had a chance to explore his new home, he will be ready for a meal.

You may well find that the pup picks at his food and then wanders away from it. This is nothing to worry about. He is just too interested in his new surroundings to settle down to eating. Give him about 10 minutes to eat as much as he wants, and then remove the bowl and dispose of the food. The

Littermates are used to being fed together, and, initially, your pup will miss the rivalry of eating with his brothers and sisters.

Stick to the diet your puppy is accustomed to – at least to begin with.

pup will probably have more appetite when his next meal is due, but some pups take a couple of days to re-find their enthusiasm for food. As long as your pup appears fit and well, there is no cause for concern. Make sure fresh drinking water is available, and feed fresh food at every meal.

However, if your pup is refusing his food and also appears to be off-colour – for example, showing signs of diarrhoea or constipation – consult your vet.

FADDY FEEDERS

If a pup is not keen on his food, the temptation is to try something new in the hope that he will like it better. This is a flawed plan for several reasons.

- It is advisable to stick to the diet the pup is used to in order to avoid digestive upsets. A sudden change is a classic cause of diarrhoea.
- In most cases, the breeder will have found a diet that suits the breed, and it is best to be guided by their experience.
- A pup who is being tempted by new food may well get more and more picky in the knowledge that you will keep trying to find him something that is even more tasty!

The complete diets that are designed for growing puppies and for adults cater for nutritional requirements, but they are not always highly palatable. Before you think about changing diets, you can work at making the food more appetising for the dog. This can be done by mixing in gravy, or by adding a small amount of chicken as an incentive.

You will probably find that, once your pup has settled, he is more than ready to eat his food without any added encouragement. Remember, if you are feeding a complete diet, it is nutritionally balanced to suit the needs of the dog. Supplements should not be added, as this will upset the balance of the diet.

CHANGING DIETS

If there is a pressing reason why you should change diets, such as a problem with supply, or if the diet is upsetting your puppy, make the changeover as gradual as possible, to avoid stomach upsets. Begin by mixing in a little of the new food at every meal, and, over a period of days, you can make a complete switch.

Your pup will soon learn to love his indoor kennel.

INDOOR KENNEL TRAINING

If you are planning to use an indoor kennel, you will need to train your pup to go into it and to learn to settle. This is not as difficult as it sounds, as even the most energetic pup gets tired and wants to find a place where he can rest undisturbed.

- Make the indoor kennel as attractive as possible, lining it with fleecy bedding, and maybe providing a toy.
- If the indoor kennel looks very big, you can use a cardboard box as a bed (see page 48), and place it in the kennel.
- Some owners drape a rug or a blanket over the top and sides of the indoor kennel, which makes it look even more cosy and den-like.
- Encourage your pup to go into his indoor kennel. You can throw a toy or a treat through the door, and the puppy should follow it inside.
- Once the pup is in the indoor kennel, praise him and stroke him, leaving the door open. Keep the pup occupied for a few minutes, playing with him and rewarding him, before allowing him out.
- When your pup appears to be tired, take him to his indoor kennel, repeat the above exercise, and then close the door. Do not leave the room

immediately, or your pup will think he is being deserted.
- Stay quietly in the room for a few minutes, reading the newspaper or getting on with the washing up. Do not pay any attention if your pup whines or barks.
- Hopefully the pup will quickly realise that making a fuss is getting him nowhere, and, if he is sufficiently tired, he will settle.

It may take some time for your pup to learn to settle, and you will need to work at building up the length of time he stays in the indoor kennel. It may help if you feed your pup in the indoor kennel with the door open, as this will build up a pleasurable association.

POINTS TO REMEMBER
- The indoor kennel should only be used for limited periods in the daytime, such as when you cannot supervise him or if you have to go on a short outing and cannot take your pup.
- The indoor kennel must *never* be used for punishment.
- Do not make a big fuss of your pup when you are putting him in the indoor kennel or when you are releasing him, as this will get him hyped up about being left alone (see page 123).
- Resist the temptation of coming to check on your puppy or trying to prevent him whining or barking. You are only teaching the pup *not* to settle.
- Do not give up with the indoor kennel because your pup does not settle at once. In the overwhelming number of cases, the pup learns to love his indoor kennel, and most adult dogs are happy to go in there to rest when the door is left open.

HOUSE-TRAINING
House-training will be a top priority over the next few weeks, but you should get into a routine from the moment your pup arrives home. The fewer 'accidents' he has in the house, the quicker he will

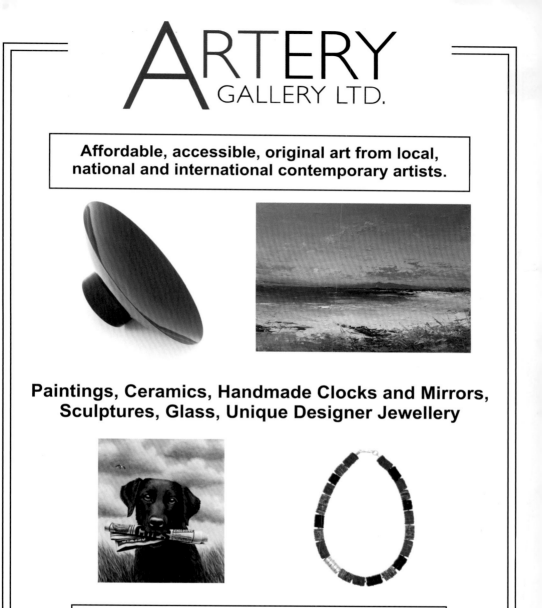

ARTERY
GALLERY LTD.

(handwritten, upper left) David Connolly / Wolfspeak fodvath / Kenlock

Artery Gallery, based in St Andrews, is a leader amongst contemporary art galleries, having gathered together a wonderfully eclectic range of unique art and craft from local, national and international artists, both emerging and already established.

The aim of Artery Gallery is to make art more affordable and accessible, through a friendly, welcoming environment, offering everyone the opportunity to own something original and handmade by a person instead of a production line.

Many of our customers had never been into a gallery before coming to Artery and now return time after time, bringing their families and friends. You can also keep abreast of the latest additions to our collections through our user- friendly, secure website.

Visitors from further a field can have their purchases delivered if travelling lightly, and there is a worldwide tax free service available.

We also operate a gift registration service for weddings and civil partnerships and Artery gift vouchers are available up to any value.

We could tell you about the gorgeous designer jewellery, or the stunning seascapes; the funky metal panels and clocks; the amazing ceramics from Crete; or the beautiful collection of glass…but instead… why not come in and see for yourself?

Where To Find Us:

43 South Street, St Andrews, Fife, KY16 9QR
Tel: 01334 478 221

Open Monday – Friday 10am to 5pm
Saturday 10am to 5.30pm
Sunday 12pm to 4pm (Seasonal)

E-mail: info@arteryuk.com

Registered in Scotland No.271628. Registered Office: 43 South Street, St Andrews, Fife, KY16 9QR
VAT Registered No.845 6229 10

If you are vigilant, your pup will soon learn to be clean in the house.

learn that he should relieve himself in the garden.

The key to successful house-training is consistency. If you take your pup to the same area in the garden, use the same command, and take your pup out at regular, routine intervals, he will soon get the idea. Your pup will need to go out at the following times:

- When he wakes up after sleep.
- After a meal.
- After a play session.
- First thing in the morning.
- Last thing at night.
- If you see him sniffing or circling.

Never go for longer than two hours without allowing your pup access to the garden.

STEP BY STEP

- Take your pup into the area of the garden you have chosen for toiletting, and give a verbal command. Guide Dog puppy walkers teach their pups to be "Busy", but you can use any command you like, as long as you are happy about the neighbours overhearing!
- The moment your pup 'performs' use the command, and, in time, he will learn to associate the command with the action.
- Give lots of praise, and your pup will understand that he has responded correctly.
- Have a short game with your pup before taking him back into the house. If you go in directly your pup has performed, he may adopt delaying tactics so he can stay out longer.

BONUS POINTS

The big advantage of training a dog to relieve himself on command is that you can prepare for an outing and be confident that your dog will not need to relieve himself in a public place. However, you should always act on the principle of better safe than sorry, and make sure you carry the means to clean up after your dog if necessary.

WHEN ACCIDENTS HAPPEN

No matter how vigilant you are, it is inevitable that your pup will have the odd accident. The most important point to remember it that, nine times out of ten, it is your fault for failing to see the warning signs.

Never reprimand your puppy if you discover a mess. Unless you catch the pup red-handed, he will have absolutely no idea why you are displeased. He will associate your displeasure with whatever he was doing a couple of seconds previously, not with something he may have done 20 minutes before. The old-fashioned idea that a pup will learn if you rub his nose in the mess has no substance, and will only result in a confused and bewildered puppy.

If you find your pup has had an accident, clean it up thoroughly, making sure you use a deodoriser. If you are not scrupulous in cleaning up, there is a risk of the pup deciding that this is a favourite spot to use.

If you catch your pup in the act, or spot him circling and sniffing, do not yell at him! Take him outside to his toilet area as quickly as possible and give the verbal command to be clean. When your pup responds, be quick to praise him, putting his earlier slip-up out of your mind.

AT NIGHT

A young puppy cannot be expected to be clean at night to begin with, but there are ways to hasten the process. A pup does not want to foul his sleeping quarters, and so you need to allocate an area where he can relieve himself.

If you are using an indoor kennel, line the front with newspaper, so the pup does not have to soil his bedding. The pup will use this area if he needs to, but he will soon learn to wait until he is released from his indoor kennel.

If you do not have an indoor kennel, it may take slightly longer for the pup to be clean through the night, as can put some distance between his bed and the place where he fouls. The best plan is to put newspaper down, so that your pup learns to use this. Remember to let your puppy out last thing at night and the moment you wake in the morning, and he will soon get the message.

COMMON MISTAKES

House-training is a straightforward business, and can be achieved swiftly and effectively if the owner is prepared to work hard in the first few weeks.

The most common mistake is to expect a pup to relieve himself just because you have let him out into the garden. In most cases, the pup will take the opportunity to explore the garden or dig a hole, and it is a matter of luck whether he relieves himself.

It is your job to take the pup to his designated toilet area, to give the verbal command, and to stay with him (rain or shine) until he performs. In this way, the pup knows exactly why he is being taken out, and he will waste no time in doing what is required.

Another common error is to cease to be so punctilious about taking your pup out as he matures. Obviously, he will not need to go out so frequently, but, for the first six months, you will still need to do the thinking for him and take him out at regular intervals.

An adult dog may well learn to ask to be let out by sitting at the door, but it is better to provide regular opportunities rather than relying on the dog to attract your attention.

SETTLING AT NIGHT

The first day in a new home is an exhausting experience for a puppy, and it would be logical if the pup fell into a long, deep sleep. However, pups rarely see it this way. After a stressful day in a new environment, the pup is keen to keep his new family in his sights. When he is suddenly deserted at night, he finds untapped energy to voice his protests – and some pups can be very persistent!

How do you get through the first night – and, indeed, the nights to come? The answer is, to make up your mind as to how to deal with your puppy and stick to it. If you are quite happy to have a dog sleeping upstairs, or even on your bed, that is okay as long as you make the decision. Do not make the mistake of giving into your pup "just for the first night", or "just for the first few days". You will end up with a dog who refuses to settle unless he has company.

In most situations, it is preferable for the dog to sleep in his own designated area. It is more hygienic

Your pup may appear to be tired, but that does not mean that he will settle to sleep at night!

than sharing a bed, and it teaches the dog to be self-sufficient for a set period of time. Guide dog puppies are always trained to stay in their own sleeping quarters.

- Feed the last meal of the day between 8-9pm. A young pup has a small stomach, and if he has too long to wait until breakfast, he will have a good reason to protest.
- In the summer, it gets light very early, so take steps to block out the light, if necessary, or your pup will thinks it's time to get up at 4am!
- At bedtime, take your pup to his toilet area in the garden and wait until he relieves himself. Have a quick game in the hope of tiring him out completely.
- Settle the pup in his sleeping quarters, tempting him into his bed or his indoor kennel with a treat.
- If you are not using an indoor kennel, check that

the room is free of all potential hazards so that you can be confident about leaving him.
- Provide a toy to keep the pup occupied, first ensuring that the pup can come to no harm if he chews it. A boredom-busting toy, filled with tiny food treats, is an excellent distraction.
- Now shut the door, and leave your puppy. Go to bed, and use ear plugs if necessary!

It is inevitable that the pup will protest, but it is important to resist the temptation of checking up on him. The pup will be quick to learn that a vocal protest brings him exactly what he wants – you! Harden your heart to the pup's cries, and he will eventually settle.

The first night will be the hardest, but within a few days the pup will become accustomed to his bedtime routine. He will accept that he is left alone at night but that you are always there, first thing in the morning, ready to serve him breakfast!

CHAPTER FIVE

EARLY LEARNING

Within a couple of days, your puppy will settle into his new home. As he becomes familiar with his surroundings and gets to know his new family, he will become more confident and his personality will begin to emerge. This is a crucial period for both you and your puppy. It is the time to establish a strong bond so that the puppy learns to trust you and to accept you as his leader.

UNDERSTANDING LEADERSHIP

The old school of dog training was very keen on owners adopting an authoritarian relationship with their dogs, laying down the law and using punishment as a means of correction. Thankfully, we have moved away from this approach, and the emphasis is on motivating a dog to do as he is asked and then rewarding him. However, it is important to bear in mind that although training methods may change over a period of time, the mental make-up of a dog does not.

The dog is a direct descendant of the wolf, and, fortunately for us, he still retains many wolf-like characteristics. The domesticated dog still acts as though he is a member of a pack, and this makes the job of training so much easier.

In a wild wolf pack, the cubs are cared for, and disciplined, by their mother. As they grow older, they establish their own relationships within the pack, learning to accept the authority of adults that are superior in status. As the cubs mature into adults, they may seek to challenge this authority, but they will quickly learn their own position in the pack. At the head of the pack is the leader, and his authority is undisputed, unless he is old and weak (when his position is usurped by a younger, stronger animal).

The domesticated dog is ready to accept a human as his pack leader, and will be content to live as a pack member. However, for this relationship to work, there are a number of criteria that must be observed.

Every dog needs a leader he can respect.

The dog must be presented with clear leadership so that he understands who is in control.
This does not mean you have to be a stern disciplinarian, barking commands at your dog. But you must give a clear message so your dog learns to respect your authority. If he accepts you as a firm but fair leader, he will be content with his lower-ranking status, and will not seek to challenge your leadership.

You must be consistent in the way you behave towards your dog.
One of the most common mistakes in training is inconsistency. If you keep changing your mind about what is allowed, your dog will quickly become confused, and will start to make up his own mind about what he should or shouldn't do.

Your dog must learn that he is a valued member of the pack but that he is inferior in status to all members of the human family – including children.
If you have small children, they may not play a part in training the dog, but he must still learn to respect them. He will understand that the children are not as high-ranking as the leader of his new pack, but his behaviour must be acceptable when he is around them.

COMMUNICATING
Dogs and people do not speak the same language, but there are three ways in which we can communicate very successfully.

TOUCH
A dog likes to be stroked and petted – a pleasurable sensation that he quickly learns to associate with praise. Remember to use it when you are training your pup, when you want to give him reassurance and boost his confidence, or simply when he is sitting by your side, being a perfect companion.

VOICE
Dogs learn to associate the sound of a word with an action. In truth, it makes no difference whether you say "Sit" or "Bananas" as long as you always use the

A dog must have a clear understanding of his place in the family.

same word. The dog is responding to the sound, not the meaning. Over a period of time, some dogs build up an extensive repertory of verbal commands they respond to. This depends on the skill of the trainer as well as the intelligence of the dog.

However, there is a highly significant factor that governs all our verbal communication with dogs, and that is tone of voice. The dog has an acute sense of hearing, far superior to our own, and he will be very sensitive to the way verbal commands are given.

When you are training your puppy, use a light but firm tone of voice. Sound warm and encouraging as your pup starts to co-operate, and go over the top when you praise him, so that he is in no doubt that he has done the right thing.

If your pup is misbehaving and you want to interrupt his behaviour, make your voice deep and gruff. There is no need to shout – your pup can hear perfectly well – it is a matter of whether he chooses to respond!

BODY LANGUAGE

This method of communicating is hugely important in the animal world, but we tend to pay it scant attention. A dog will be totally clued into the way his owner moves, and this will affect his own responses. For example, if you command your dog to "Stay" and step a few paces away from him, you need to ensure that you are giving the correct visual message to back up the verbal command. While the dog is in the Stay position, you must avoid eye contact and keep your body as still as possible, so that he has no encouragement to move.

In contrast, if you want your pup to come to you, you want to support a verbal command with exciting body language – arms wide open, even jumping up and down – so that the dog really wants to come to you.

As your dog becomes more attuned to you, he will sense your mood even if you have not said a word to him or to anyone else. It is this special sensitivity that makes the dog such a rewarding companion.

MOTIVATION

Why should your puppy do as you ask? If you take on the role of leader, your pup will learn to respect you, and may actively seek to win your approval. However, a lively young puppy also has his own agenda of interests he wishes to pursue. Why should he come back to you if he is having fun with another dog? Why should he give up his toy when he wants to play with it? A puppy may respond because he is frightened of being reprimanded, but a far more effective method of training is for the pup to respond because he wants to. That means offering a reward that he is prepared to work for. The pup will be so keen to get the reward that he is willing to change his behaviour.

A dog needs to be motivated – and rewarded – for co-operating with you.

The key is to find a reward that motivates your pup so highly that he will put all other considerations aside. Food is very often the answer. If a pup knows you have a treat, he will generally bend over backwards for it. It is a good idea to find out what your pup likes best, and then you can grade the treat according to the situation. Most dogs will work for the type of treat you can buy commercially, but there are times when you may want to step up the ante and offer a treat that is really enticing. Cheese, sausage and cooked liver treats are generally high-rankers, and these can be reserved for special occasions. For example:

- When you are teaching a new exercise.
- When you are working in a situation with a lot of distractions (such as a training class).
- For recalls when your dog is off-lead in a place that is full of interesting scents, or where he has other dogs to play with.

RATIONING

If you are training with treats, you must be careful not to overfeed your dog, particularly if you have a Toy breed that does not need vast quantities of food. The best plan is to work out how much food you are using for training, and then subtract it from your puppy's daily ration.

Some dogs, particularly those with a strong working instinct (e.g. the Border Collie), may be more motivated by a toy than by a food treat. Find a toy that your puppy really likes and then keep it especially for training sessions. In this way the toy has a special value, and your pup will be highly motivated to work for it when you are training.

TIMING

It sounds easy to get your timing right when you are training your dog. However, it is one of the areas where communications most frequently break down. The human brain has the ability to connect an action with a reaction over an extended period of time. A child will understand if he is being told off for a misdeed committed hours, or even days,

earlier. A dog's association time is literally a matter of seconds.

As we have seen with house-training (page 62), it is pointless to chastise a puppy for an accident that may have occurred 30 minutes previously. In the same way, you cannot be angry at your pup when he eventually responds to the recall after spending some time sniffing around. In his mind, he is not being told off for the delay, he is being told off for coming to you.

Exactly the same formula applies to praising a dog. You must give praise at the moment your pup is responding correctly, not when he has jumped up and broken his Stay, or when he has pulled ahead after completing a few steps of perfect heelwork. As far as the dog is concerned, you are expressing approval when he broke his Stay or when he pulled ahead.

When you are training, 'think dog' and make your timing complement the dog's association time.

AWAKENING INSTINCTS

The dog's instinct to be a member of a pack works very much to our advantage, but there are other forms of instinctive behaviour that may not prove to be such an asset. As we have seen in Chapter 2, selective breeding has created breeds with specialised skills, and some of these working instincts remain very strong. This is good news if you want a Border Collie to herd sheep, but it can be a menace if your pet dog becomes obsessed with rounding up footballs or chasing bicycles.

The skill of the dog owner is to awaken the instincts that are desirable, and to allow other instincts, which may produce inappropriate behaviour, to lie dormant. If an instinct is stimulated, it will become stronger and stronger. If it is not kindled, it will fade through lack of use. Therefore, you must work out what is likely to encourage a particular instinct, and then control the situation accordingly.

Guide dogs are trained to work closely with a blind or partially sighted owner, and so a firm check must be kept on instinctive behaviour that is likely

This is an effective method of training pioneered by Karen Pryor, based in the USA. She started clicker training when she was working with dolphins, but her methods work successfully with all animals.

The dog (or whatever animal you are training) is taught to associate the sound of the clicker with getting a reward. He then learns to 'earn' his click by offering the behaviour that you want. The click acts as a 'yes' marker, telling the dog he has done the right thing and signalling that a reward will follow.

The great advantage of the clicker is that you can be very precise with your timing, marking the exact moment when your dog is offering the correct behaviour, rather than the rather woolly "Good dog", and rewarding some time after the dog has behaved correctly.

At Guide Dogs, puppy walking supervisors may use clicker training in certain circumstances to help a puppy walker to overcome a particular problem, or in a group training situation. Some trainers use the clicker when dogs come in for advanced training. The clicker may be helpful if a dog is struggling to master a particular exercise, or simply to speed up or sharpen his responses. It is important that a trainee guide dog does not become reliant on this method of training, and a skilled trainer will know when it is time to relinquish the aid.

If you are interested in trying clicker training, the best plan is to find a club that specialises in this method. You will then be given help on getting your timing right and on using the clicker in the most effective way. There are also a number of books and videos that give guidance on clicker training.

Clicker training is based on positive reinforcement and it has proved to be a most effective method of training – as long as you get your timing right...

A guide dog must be focused on his work, and instinctive behaviour, such as chasing, needs to be suppressed.

If the instinct to chase is not encouraged, it is more likely to lie dormant.

to prejudice their work. For example, most retriever breeds will instinctively chase a ball, or run after a toy that is thrown and bring it back. This is no problem as long as the instinct to run and retrieve does not become too strong, which would be disastrous in a working guide dog. Puppy walkers are aware of this potential problem, and so ball games and retrieve games are always controlled and limited.

In contrast, the puppies that are trained to be assistance dogs for Dogs for the Disabled or Canine Partners are actively encouraged to retrieve, as this will form a major part of their task work when they are working with a disabled owner.

A small number of Border Collies are used as guide dogs, and puppy walkers are aware of the danger of encouraging the instinct to chase and to herd, which are so integral to the breed. Playing football, or any other ball game, will stimulate these instincts, and, with the Border Collie's somewhat

obsessive nature, you will soon end up with a dog who can think about nothing more than the next ball game.

German Shepherd Dogs are valued by the police and security services for their strong guarding instinct, but this is not required for guide dog work. German Shepherds make successful guide dogs as long as the instinct to guard people or possessions is diluted so that it has no effect on the dog's behaviour.

PLAYING GAMES

Awakening instincts in a dog is often unintentional, and it can frequently happen through play. No one would wish to discourage play sessions with a puppy; it is a good way of building up a bond as well as having fun together. However, it is important to be aware of the type of behaviour you are encouraging. This is particularly relevant if you have children in the family who will play without thinking of the possible consequences.

Start as you mean to go on, so your pup understands what is expected of him.

Think before you play, bearing in mind the following guidelines:

- Do not go overboard with tug games, particularly if you have a medium- to large-size breed. These games can quickly get out of hand, and the pup learns to pit his strength against you. This type of game should never be played with Staffordshire Bull Terriers or Bull Terriers, which retain some of the instincts from their fighting past.
- Make sure it is you – rather than the puppy – who decides to end the game. A pup who always runs off with his toy will soon learn that he can dictate proceedings, and this will have an adverse effect on his training.
- When you are ready to end the game, ask the dog to "Give" the toy (see page 78), and then put it out of reach. The dog must learn that you 'own' the toys and

DO NOT ALLOW YOUR PUPPY TO:

- Sleep on the bed.
- Climb up on the furniture.
- Beg when you are eating (this applies to snacks as well as to mealtimes when you are eating at the table).
- Guard his food bowl, his toys, or his sleeping quarters (see page 120).
- Barge through doorways, putting himself ahead of you (see page 120).
- Jump up at adults or children.
- Play-bite adults or children (see page 77).
- Bark excessively.
- Chase small children.
- Chase the cat.
- Show too much interest in caged pets.

This may appear to be a long list of don'ts, but once your pup understands what is acceptable, he will not seek to challenge you or the rules you have laid down.

you decide when to play with them. A dog with a strong guarding instinct, such as a Rottweiler or a Bullmastiff, can become possessive about toys (see page 120).

- Depending on the breed of puppy, make sure you limit ball games so the puppy does not become obsessed by chasing or herding.

GETTING STARTED

From the moment your puppy comes home, you will be building your relationship with him. Use every opportunity to show your puppy how you want him to behave, and remember to reward him every time he co-operates. At this age, a puppy is eager to please and to win your approval. Make the most of this time, and you will be amazed at how quickly a young pup will learn.

FIRST WORDS

Hopefully, you will have chosen a name for your pup before he arrives home (see page 50). Make sure you use it every time you want to attract the puppy's attention and every time you praise him. In this way, the pup will develop a pleasurable association with the sound of his name. It will signal the time he interacts with people, and he will enjoy being the focus of attention. Call the pup by his 'proper' name, e.g. "Sam", to begin with. If you introduce too many variations, such as "Sammy", "Sampson", "Samuel", etc., the pup will get confused. In most cases, a pup will have learnt his name by the end of his first day in his new home.

The second word that will be picked up in record time is "No!" As a pup explores his surroundings and interacts with members of the family – both human and animal – he is finding out what is acceptable behaviour. A pup does not *know* it is wrong to investigate the kitchen bin or to bite your fingers, he has to *learn*.

Initially, the command "No" will not mean anything to an inquisitive pup, so you will need to follow it up by attracting his attention, and then rewarding him when he is concentrating on you. For example, if your pup tries to jump up on the sofa, say "No" in a firm voice, and then tempt him to come to you by showing him a toy. Make it look as if there is a really good game on offer, and then give lots of praise when the pup stops trying to climb on to the sofa and comes towards you. Remember to keep your half of the bargain and have a quick game with your pup – no matter how busy you are – otherwise he won't fall for your ploy another time.

HOUSE RULES

You and your family should decide what is, and what is not, allowed – and then stick to it. If you are rearing a companion dog, this is a matter of personal choice; you can decide whether you want your dog to sleep on the furniture or not. But whatever you decide, you must be 100 per cent consistent in applying the rules. A pup will not understand that he is allowed on the sofa except when he is wet and muddy. As far as he is concerned, you have allowed him to go on the sofa, and he will be baffled by your sudden, and to him, inexplicable change of mind.

A guide dog puppy must be a model housedog so that he will fit in with his blind owner and family with the minimum disruption. You may not wish to observe all the following house rules, but they make a good guide if you want to rear a well-behaved, adaptable dog.

HANDLING

It is essential that your puppy is accustomed to being handled all over.

This is important for grooming, for veterinary examinations, and to show the dog that you have a right to handle him (rather than allowing 'no go' areas to develop). It also provides an opportunity to get to know your dog. If you are familiar with his physical appearance and condition, you will spot any signs of trouble at an early stage. This could make a crucial difference if a health problem was to develop.

Hopefully, the breeder will have handled the puppies in the litter on a regular basis, so your pup will have some idea of what is required. At Guide

HANDLING

Start by running your hand over the pup's body, along the back and along his tummy.

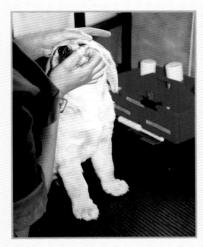

Check the eyes.

Lift up each paw in turn.

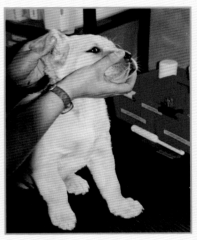

Examine the ears.

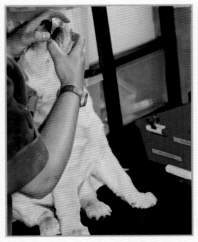

Open the mouth and examine the teeth and gums.

Lift the pup on to his hindlegs to check his underside.

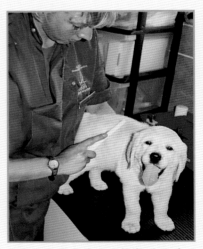

Run a brush through the coat.

Dogs, each puppy is given a thorough examination before being placed with a puppy walker, and the routine that is used in kennels serves as a useful guide.

- Stand your puppy on the floor or a table (provided it has a non-slip surface). You can use a rubber mat to ensure the puppy does not slip.
- Run your hands over the puppy's body, starting at the head and working along the back through to the tail. The pup will get used to the touch of your hands, and you can check to make sure there are no unusual lumps or bumps, or areas where the pup is over-sensitive.
- When the pup is standing, lift his tail and encourage him to stand still. This type of handling will be needed if the vet has to take the dog's temperature.
- Pick up each paw in turn. Check the pads for cuts or soreness. They should feel soft to the touch (not too leathery).
- Look at the nails and make sure that they are even in length, with no signs of splitting. If the nails have grown too long, they will need to be trimmed (see page 77).
- Look in each of the ears. The inside should be clean and smell fresh. If there is superficial dirt, you can clean the ear with cotton wool. If the ear is red, inflamed, or foul-smelling, you should consult a vet.
- Examine the eyes. They should be wide open and clear, with no sign of discharge. The inner eyelid should not be visible.

Teach your pup to give up his toy on request.

- Open the mouth and check the gums and teeth. The gums should be pink and healthy, the teeth should be clean with no build-up of tartar, and the breath should smell fresh. Regular tooth-brushing is often necessary as the dog matures, so it is a good idea to get your pup used to this routine.
- Look at the nose. The nostrils should be open and free from discharge. A cold, wet nose is not necessarily an indication of good health – it is more a sign that the dog continually licks his nose!
- Lift the pup so that he is standing on his hindlegs. This will allow you to check his underside and the genital area. The genitals should be clean, with no evidence of soreness or discharge.
- Run a brush or a comb lightly through the coat. The coat should be clean and shiny, with no sign or flea dirt or dandruff.

To begin with, your pup may wriggle and try to bite your hands, but if you are firm with your handling, giving plenty of praise when the pup co-operates, he will quickly learn to accept the attention.

GROOMING
Puppies do not require much grooming, but they should get used to the feel of a brush and a comb, and they must also learn to keep still. If you have chosen a longcoated breed, such as a Shih Tzu or a Rough Collie, it is essential that the pup learns to love his grooming sessions, as they will be part of his daily life.

The best method to accustom your pup to regular grooming is to start with very short sessions, and to reward him with a treat or a game with a toy when he has co-operated for a couple of minutes. Once he is used to this, you can then work at building up the amount of time your dog spends on the grooming table.

NAIL TRIMMING
This is a straightforward procedure, but some dogs can become very wary of the nail-clippers. Often,

this is because a nail has been cut too short, causing the quick to bleed. Although this is not serious, it is uncomfortable, and is certainly enough to give a dog bad associations with the nail-clippers.

If you are uncertain about trimming nails, ask the vet or a nurse at the veterinary practice to show you what to do. When you are confident, you can take on the task yourself. It may be helpful if you have someone to help you hold the puppy, so that you can concentrate on the job in hand. Reassure your puppy while you are working, and give him a treat when you have finished so that he learns that it is worth his while to co-operate.

TEETH CLEANING
Your pup may initially object to having his mouth opened, but once you introduce meaty-flavoured toothpaste, he will cease to object. The toothpaste can be applied with a fingerbrush or with a long-handled brush, depending on which you find easier. Be firm if your pup tries to struggle, and remember to reward him when you have finished.

PLAY BITING
Puppies explore the world using their eyes, their ears, their sense of smell, and their mouths. In the nest, the young puppies develop these senses over a period of weeks, and you can chart their growing skills when you watch the puppies play together. The pups play by chasing each other, rolling over and biting at whichever bit of anatomy they can reach. A smaller, weaker pup may whimper if he is bowled over by a bigger pup, and if a pup gets too boisterous with his mother, he will receive a swift reprimand. But in an evenly matched litter, it is pretty much a free for all.

When a puppy joins his new human pack, he is still governed by the manners he learnt in the litter. He wants to pick up anything that smells or looks interesting, and give it a good chew. The problem arises when the pup decides that your fingers fall into this category. Nearly all puppies start off play-biting, so you need to put a stop to this behaviour before it becomes established.

Until the age of around four months, a puppy will still have his milk teeth. These are like little needles, and although they cannot do real damage, they can give a painful nip. This is obviously undesirable, particularly if you have small children who may become frightened. A child may cry out, grabbing their hand away, and the pup is more than likely to see this as part of the game, becoming over-excited as the cries get louder.

The best plan is to tackle the problem from the moment your pup arrives home. There are two areas to work on:

POSITIVE TRAINING
- Start off by offering the pup a treat. If the pup tries to grab it, close your fist over the treat, and use the command "Gently".
- Offer the treat again; if the pup grabs again, repeat the procedure outlined above.
- The moment your pup shows an improvement, reward him with the treat.
- Work on this several times a day, withholding the treat until the pup is taking it nicely.
- You can apply the same exercise when you are playing with toys. Offer the pup a toy, and do not let him have it until he takes it quietly and calmly.
- When the game is finished, ask the pup to "Give" the toy. He will probably be reluctant, so be ready to substitute the toy with a treat so he is rewarded for co-operating.
- Offer the toy again and repeat the exercise so that the pup learns that if he gives up his toy, it does not always mean that he has lost it for good.

NEGATIVE TRAINING
Training your pup to take toys and treats gently is a way of controlling interactions so that the pup learns he must behave in the way that you want in order to get his reward.

Obviously, there will be times when the pup gets carried away when you are handling or playing with him, and he will take your fingers in his mouth. This must be corrected instantly.
- If your pup bites, bellow "Ow!" in a deep, gruff voice. This will surprise your puppy, and, in most cases, he will release your fingers.
- Immediately offer a toy so that your pup has something that he is allowed to bite.
- Let him chew the toy for a few minutes, and then take it from him, using the command "Give".
- If you continue to experience problems with play-biting, you may consider using training discs as a way of interrupting the behaviour (see page 121).

Do not get angry with your pup, or feel concerned that biting may be a sign of poor temperament. The puppy is behaving instinctively, and it is your job to teach the pup to adapt his behaviour so it is acceptable in a human pack.

TEETHING TROUBLES
When your puppy starts to get his second set of teeth, the tendency to chew and bite will increase. Sometimes a puppy will go through teething with

Teething can be a troublesome time and it may affect ear carriage.

scarcely any problems, but others suffer with sore and inflamed gums, and have a great need to chew as the new teeth erupt. Teething can also affect ear carriage. Dogs with erect ears, such as German Shepherds, can go very lop-sided, with one ear up and one down during the teething process.

Be careful when handling your puppy's mouth during this time, as he will be more sensitive. Keep a regular check to ensure that the milk teeth are falling out without undue difficulty and the adult teeth are coming through correctly. In some of the Toy breeds, the adult teeth sometimes push through before the milk teeth have been shed, in which case you will need to seek veterinary advice.

Provide your pup with safe chew toys so that he has something that he can gnaw on. A marrow bone, or a sterilised bone filled with meaty paste are useful options, as long as the pup is supervised.

OPPORTUNITY TRAINING

Training a puppy is a continuous business, and you may be teaching important lessons even though you are not conducting a formal training session. This is true of all situations where you are handling the puppy and when you are being consistent in enforcing house rules.

Get into the habit of using the opportunities that present themselves, so that the puppy is unconsciously gathering information and learning what is acceptable. Be quick to praise when the puppy does something you like, such as following you out of the house when you are taking him to his toilet area – even though you are not teaching him to "Come" in a formal manner. If he sits when you offer his food bowl, give him lots of praise so that he understands that you approve of what he is doing.

The aim is to interact with your puppy, praising him when he has done well and correcting him when it is necessary. In this way, the puppy becomes increasingly responsive and far more eager to please.

This pup is learning to sit quietly, even though he is not having a formal lesson.

CHAPTER SIX

BASIC EXERCISES

A Guide Dog puppy will live with his puppy walker and family for approximately 12 months. During this time, he will learn basic obedience exercises, as well as undergoing a comprehensive programme of socialisation (see Chapter 7). The exercises that are outlined apply to all pet dogs, with a few minor differences, such as the heelwork position (see page 85). The aim is to produce a calm, obedient dog, who is happy to work and is responsive to his handler.

SETTING THE SCENE

When you start training your puppy, make sure that all the odds are stacked in your favour so you have the best chance of achieving success.

- Do not attempt to train when your puppy is tired out after a hectic play session, or when he has just eaten. If you are working with food treats, these will have far more allure when he is feeling hungry!
- Choose an area that is as free from distractions as possible. When your pup gets older, you can increase the challenge by stepping up the distractions, but, in the initial stages, your pup needs to be able to concentrate on you.
- Restrict training to short sessions – just a few minutes at a time to begin with. A puppy's concentration span is very short, and you will achieve far more if you keep sessions brief rather than dragging them out until the pup is

thoroughly bored and fed up.
- Make training sessions fun, breaking up exercises with play. You want your puppy to enjoy working with you.
- Always end a training session on a good note so that the puppy feels confident and happy. If he is struggling to learn an exercise, go back and do something easy so you have the opportunity to praise and reward him.
- Do not attempt to train if you are in a bad mood, or if you are short of time. Your mood will transfer to the puppy and everyone will end up with frayed nerves.

Remember, a puppy has a short concentration span.

INTERMITENT REWARDS

You will, by now, have discovered what motivates your puppy, and the reward that you give will be the key to successful training. However, it is important not to get trapped into giving a reward every time you ask your pup to do something. When he is learning a new exercise, he will need to be encouraged and rewarded at every step. But once he has mastered the exercise, the reward can be dropped off or given intermittently, so that your pup is still motivated and rewarded, but he is having to work that little bit harder.

The best analogy is to think of teaching a child to read. To begin with, you give lavish praise when the child stumbles through the ABC. But as he or she progresses, you praise when the child can read their first word, their first sentence, or their first book. It is exactly the same when training a dog. Praise and reward are essential in the early stages, but just as it would be ridiculous to praise a child who can read fluently for reciting their ABC, there is no need to reward a dog every time he sits on command.

Never train without rewards, but make sure your pup has worked for his treat, and then he will value it far more.

SIT

This is the easiest exercise to teach, and you will be rewarded by almost instant success.

- Get your puppy's attention and show him that you have a treat in your hand.
- Hold the treat just above his nose so that he has to look up. Wait a few seconds, with your hand held still, and the pup will lower his hindquarters to go into the Sit.
- As he goes into the correct position, give the command "Sit" and then praise him and give him the treat.
- Repeat the exercise a couple more times, and then have a game.
- If your puppy is slow to catch on, you can apply gentle pressure on his hindquarters to encourage him to Sit – although most puppies do not need

The Sit is the easiest exercise to teach.

this extra help.
- You can get in an extra lesson at mealtimes, holding the food bowl just above your puppy's head and then asking him to "Sit".
- As soon as the puppy has linked the verbal command "Sit" with the correct response, you will not need to lure him into position with a treat.
- Practise giving the Sit command in a variety of situations, and reward intermittently.

TRAINING TIP

It is all too easy to get into the habit of repeating a command in the hope that the pup will eventually make up his mind to respond. Instead of the crisp command "Shep, Sit", you are endlessly repeating "Shep, Sit, Sit, Sit…", and the pup takes no notice of you. When you give a command, always count to five before you repeat it. If your pup fails to respond, introduce an additional aid (such as gentle pressure on the hindquarters to encourage the dog to sit) so that your pup learns to respond promptly to a command.

Use a treat to lure your pup into the Down.

DOWN

This is an extension of the Sit exercise, and although some puppies take slightly longer to learn the correct position, it does not pose any real problems.

- Ask your puppy to Sit, and show him that you have a treat in your hand.
- Close your hand over the treat, and lower it to the floor.
- The pup will follow the movement of your hand (and the smell of the treat), and his head will come down to floor level.
- Keep your hand in position, with your palm closed over the treat. After a few moments, your

pup will drop his forequarters in his efforts to get at the treat.
- If you are lucky, his hindquarters will follow, and your pup will be in the Down position. Give the command "Down", praise and reward.
- If your pup is reluctant to go into the Down position, you can apply gentle pressure to the shoulder, and then praise and reward as soon as the puppy goes into the correct position.
- Repeat the exercise, using the verbal command, so that the pup associates the command with the action.
- As your pup progresses, wait a little longer before giving the reward so that your pup learns to maintain the position.
- To begin with, you will need to crouch at the puppy's side and lure him into position. But as he progresses, you will be able to stand after giving the command, and the pup will stay in position.
- In time, you will be able to give the verbal command when you are standing, and you will not need to lure the puppy or reward him every time he responds correctly.

TRAINING TIP

It is useful to have a release word, such as "Okay" so that your pup knows when an exercise is finished. It is important that you decide when the dog breaks position, rather than the dog getting up when he thinks he has done all that is required.

PUTTING ON A COLLAR

Your puppy can get used to wearing his collar as soon as he has settled in his new home. If you have bought a soft, lightweight collar, your pup will hardly know that he has got it on.

- Fasten the collar round the puppy's neck, ensuring you can fit two fingers under the collar when it is fastened.
- Distract the pup with a game or by giving him a treat. He may stop and scratch at the collar, but he will forget it if you make the game more interesting.
- You can put the collar on just before a mealtime. The puppy will be so busy eating, that he will take no notice of his collar.
- Gradually extend the length of time your pup wears his collar until he is happy to have it on all the time.

ATTACHING THE LEAD

When your pup is accustomed to wearing his collar, you can take the next step and attach his lead. Although you may not be taking your puppy out on a lead until he has completed his vaccinations, you can use the time to work on lead training.

- Attach the lead to the collar, and let it trail, making sure it cannot get snagged on anything.
- Pick up the lead, and follow your puppy wherever he wants to go. At this stage, he will scarcely realise that you are holding the end of his lead.
- Now encourage the pup to walk with you on the lead rather than choosing his own route. Show him a toy or a treat, and hold it out for him to follow.
- Give lots of encouragement, and praise and reward if the puppy takes just a few steps in the right direction.

Do not ask too much from your pup the first time you attach the lead.

- When your pup is walking with you, give a command such as "Heel" or "Close", but make sure you only give the command when the puppy is in the correct position.

HEELWORK POSITION

It is customary for dogs to walk to heel on the left-hand side, although this is of no great significance for the pet dog. Guide dog puppies are taught to walk just a little in front, as this will be the guiding position when they are working in harness. Regardless of whether your puppy is walking on your right side, your left side, or in front, the aim is for the pup to maintain the desired position, working on a loose lead.

It takes a lot of practice to achieve consistent heelwork, so do not be downhearted if your puppy makes slow progress. Try to keep training sessions short and light-hearted so that the pup does not feel as if he is being constantly nagged.

MAJOR PROTEST

Some puppies take major exception to the lead and go into a kangaroo routine of leaps and bounds. Do not turn this into a battle of wills, as the puppy will become hyped up and more determined to resist the lead. Try the following:

- Drop the lead and call your puppy to you. Reward him with a treat.

You will need to encourage your pup with a toy or a treat so he will walk with you.

- Play with a toy, distracting the puppy's attention until he has forgotten the lead.
- Take up the end of the lead and call the pup to you. Reward him with a treat.
- Now try a couple of steps, encouraging your pup to walk with you. He should be so focused on you that he will follow, paying no attention to the lead.
- End the session as soon as you have achieved a measure of success, no matter how small. The progress you have made means that you have something to build on when you try again.
- Keep practising in short bursts, using lots of verbal encouragement and praise, and rewarding the pup when he co-operates.

THE PULLING PUP

It is good to see a positive response when a puppy is on the lead, but you do not want this to develop into a scenario where the pup steams ahead, pulling on the lead. If you have chosen a big, strong breed, this could become a major problem.

TRAINING TIP

Many people make the mistake of giving the command "Heel" or "Close" when the puppy is pulling ahead or lagging behind, hoping to encourage the pup to come into the correct position. However, this assumes that the puppy knows where he should be – which, of course, he doesn't. The only way a puppy will learn is if you give the command when he is in the heelwork position, and by praising him if he maintains the position, walking on a loose lead.

TRAINING TIP

You can set up a training situation when you deliberately distract the pup with a ball, a food bowl, or perhaps getting someone to call him. The pup will pull to get to the object of his desires, but you must not let him reach it. Let the dog pull, and then call him back to you, rewarding him with a treat. Keep working on this, and your pup will learn that, when he pulls, he does not get any closer to what he wants. But when he responds to you, he is rewarded.

The dog is pulling towards something he wants – in this case a ball. He is allowed to get close, but he cannot reach it.

He is rewarded with a treat when he turns his back on the ball and returns to his handler.

- If your pup has a tendency to pull on the lead, do not attempt to pull him back or hang on to the lead, allowing him free reign. Some puppies react to the lead tension and will pull all the harder.
- As soon as the lead goes taut, stop, and then call your pup back to his heelwork position. Reward him for coming back to you, and then set off again, giving the command "Heel" or "Close".
- If, or rather when, the pup pulls ahead again, do exactly the same, halting, calling the pup back to you, and then setting off with the pup in the correct position.
- In time, the pup will realise that pulling is counter-productive because he keeps having to stop.

THE LAGGING PUP

In the very early stages of lead training, a pup may put the brakes on, or he may lag behind, stopping to sniff every interesting smell he comes across. If this happens, you need to make yourself as exciting as possible so that the puppy wants to be with you.

- Forget about formal heelwork to begin with. Have a good game with your pup, and get him focused on a toy.
- Without interrupting the game, walk forward a few paces, encouraging the pup to follow his toy.
- When the pup is in the heelwork position, give the verbal command, and then praise him lavishly. Play for a few moments, and then set off again.
- Keep working on this so that you build up a positive response to the lead. You can then try some turns and some changes of pace to keep the pup interested.

TRAINING TIP

Practise lead training at home so that your pup is walking confidently on the lead by the time he is ready to venture into the outside world. This means that you will be able to concentrate on socialising your pup when you take him out, rather than trying to correct his heelwork position.

STAND

This is not an essential exercise, but it can come in handy when you are grooming your dog, or if he is being examined by the vet. It is better to wait until your pup is confident in the Sit and the Down before introducing this lesson.

- Crouch down by your puppy and hold him gently by the collar.
- Stroke along the stifle joint (the hindleg 'knee' joint), which should encourage him to stand. When the pup is in the correct position, give the command "Stand".
- You can also try standing in front of the pup and holding a treat a small distance away from him. The pup will stand to reach the treat, and you can give the verbal command.
- Most pups find this exercise quite difficult, so just ask your puppy to maintain the Stand for a few moments before releasing him. Over a period of time, you can build up how long he maintains the position.

Reward your pup as soon as he goes into the Stand position.

STAY/WAIT

A puppy needs to learn to Stay in position, whether he is in the Sit, Stand or Down, until you release him. There are times, such as in the recall exercise, when you want the pup to stay in position until you call him. Some trainers use the "Wait" command for this, to differentiate it from the Stay. However, the principles of teaching the pup to maintain his position are the same.

It is better to delay teaching this exercise until your pup is working on the lead so that you will have more control. You can teach your pup to stay in the Sit, the Stand, or the Down, although it is probably easier to start with the Down, as he is most likely to settle in this position.

- Put your dog on the lead, and then command him to go "Down".

When your pup understands the Stay exercise, you can try it off-lead.

- Step one pace to the side and give the command "Stay". You can reinforce the verbal command with a hand signal – palm held flat towards the dog.
- When the puppy is in position, pause for a second, and then step back to his side. Give your release command – "Okay" – and then praise and reward.

- Try this a couple of times, and then face the pup, take a step back, and then return to the front of the dog.
- Gradually build up the distance until you can walk to the end of the lead, and the pup is happy to stay in position.
- You can try walking in a small circle around the

A NEW BREED

Vera Stokes and her husband, Gerry, wanted to take on a new challenge when they retired, and puppy walking seemed to fit the bill. They have now walked eight puppies, and all but one have qualified as guide dogs. Their current puppy is a longhaired German Shepherd called Tamara.

"We have had such lovely dogs over the years," said Vera. "We have puppy walked different breeds, but the Guide Dog breeding always shines through. You really cannot fault the temperament of the dogs they produce."

Vera has puppy walked Labradors, Labrador-Retriever crosses, Golden Retrievers, a German Shepherd, a Golden Retriever-German Shepherd cross, and, most unusually of all, a Leonberger.

"Kilo was very lollopy as a puppy, but she soon settled down," said Vera. She was not as naughty as some of our puppies, although she could be quite lively. The thing I like most about her was her gentleness – she was a really loving dog."

Kilo had few problems in training, and Vera found she had one distinct advantage over the other puppies she has walked.

"Scavenging can be a real problem. In Walsall, the streets are full of litter and discarded takeaways, and the dogs cannot resist the temptation. But a Leonberger is a proud dog; it walks with its head held high. I had no trouble with scavenging when I was walking Kilo."

Vera has always been happy to accept whatever breed is available when she is puppy walking.

"I was asked if I would like to walk the Leonberer as she was a new breed for Guide Dogs. But I have enjoyed all the different breeds. I had a very soft spot for Whisky, the German Shepherd-Retriever cross. She looked like a big Collie, with the drop ears of a Golden Retriever."

Vera and her husband are great motor caravan enthusiasts and the guide dog puppies get into the routine of spending weekends away from home at an early stage.

"When we go caravaning, the dogs get more walks, but there are periods when they have to be tied up. I am always amazed at how quickly the puppies adjust to this. You would think that they would make no end of fuss, but when they get used to the routine, they settle quite happily. In fact, it's great for socialisation as the puppies have the chance to lie quietly while they watch everything that is going on at the camp site.

"When we are at home, I take the guide dog puppy everywhere with me. We go on buses, on the metro trams, and, when the pup is coming to near the end of his time with us, I go to Birmingham on the train a couple of times."

Vera and Gerry have a resident dog at home, a Golden Retriever called Baloo.

"We puppy walked Baloo, and he was getting on really well with his advanced training. Then, when he was out with his trainer and his prospective new puppy, or you could even step over him, repeating the command "Stay". This will teach him that he must stay in position regardless of what you are doing.

• When your pup is maintaining his position consistently, take off his lead off and gradually extend the distance and the time you can leave him.

EXTENDED STAY

This may take some time before your pup fully understands what is required. The aim is to get your pup to settle in one place for an extended period of time. It is not the same as the formal Stay exercise where the dog should remain static; it is more of a social skill, teaching the dog to be quiet, not seeking attention.

owner, some boys let off some fireworks near him, and it destroyed his confidence. We were happy to have him back, and he is very kind with the new puppies."

The only member of the household who is not keen on puppy walking is the cat.

"She decided she had had enough of the puppies, and she moved next door," said Vera. "When I go to see her, she takes one look at me and leaves the room. What an insult!"

Vera finds it very hard to part with her guide dog puppies when it is time for them to go into training.

"I get so attached to them, and I can't help getting upset when they go. I thought it would get easier the more puppies I had, but I think it gets harder. I was talking to my vet and I said: 'I know this is what the puppy has been bred for, and it's what I have been working for, so why do I get so upset.' He replied: 'If you did not get so involved, you would not be doing the job properly'.

"I thought that was a very nice compliment, and I understood what

he was saying. It is hard, but it is also very rewarding when a puppy you have walked qualifies as a guide dog – even more so when you hear from the new owner and sometimes meet up."

Kilo: Now qualified as a guide dog.

The extended stay is an essential lesson for guide dog puppies to learn, as working guide dogs must settle quietly in many different situations. This might be when their owner is at work, when he/she goes to the pub or to a restaurant, or if he/she is attending a church service or some other meeting. The pet dog will not have to meet so many demands, but, even at home, it can be useful to tell a dog when it is time to lie down and be quiet.

• Wait until your pup has mastered the Down so that you can put him in a comfortable position.

• When your pup is in the Down, give the command "Stay", or you can use a different command, such as "Settle", to differentiate from the formal Stay exercise. The aim is for the puppy to relax and settle quietly, so it is a good idea to choose a time when you know the pup is tired.

• If the puppy is restless, kneel down by his side and stroke him. When he is quiet, say "Good, Stay" so that he knows he is doing what you want.

• If you are lucky, the puppy will settle, and may even go to sleep. If the pup is struggling, make sure he settles for a few minutes, and then release him. You can gradually build up the length of time he settles.

You can teach this exercise at any time, and in any place – when watching television, when waiting your turn to see the vet, or when you have friends round to visit. Eventually, you will be rewarded by having a dog that never makes a nuisance of himself at inappropriate times.

A working guide dog will be expected to settle for extended periods – but it is a useful exercise for all dogs to learn.

COME WHEN CALLED

A dog that has a strong recall is a pleasure to own, and makes life far better for the dog. If you are sure that your dog will come back, you are far more likely to allow him off-lead. Guide dogs must be 100 per cent on the recall, or they cannot work with a blind or partially sighted owner. Puppy walkers spend time training all the basic exercises, but the recall is viewed as one of the top priorities.

FIRST STEPS

When a puppy first arrives in his new home, he will follow you everywhere. This provides a golden opportunity to start recall training.

A young pup will want to be with you, so use every opportunity to call him to you.

SECRET WEAPON

Guide Dog puppy walkers are provided with a whistle, which is used for recall training.

- At mealtimes, the pup is asked to "Sit", and the whistle is blown. In this way, the pup learns to associate the sound of the whistle with food.
- When recall training starts, the whistle can be used after the verbal command "Come" has been given.
- The pup responds to the command and the whistle, and is rewarded with a treat. The strength of the association – whistle equals food – has been reinforced.
- In time, the pup will respond to the whistle alone, and, in most cases, it prompts a very swift response.

The whistle is a brilliant training aid for all dog owners, as the sound carries over long distances, and it triggers an instant reaction.

- When your pup is following you, crouch down, use his name, and give the command "Come".
- Give lots of praise when your pup comes to you. In fact, he is only doing what he wanted to do, but he is learning to associate the word "Come" with the correct response, and he is finding out that he always gets lots of fuss and attention when he comes to you.
- You can work on this exercise by having a treat ready when you call your puppy. This underlines that it is worth his while to come to you.
- Practise in the house, calling your pup from room to room. Ask someone in the family to hold on to the puppy, and then call him into the kitchen when his meal is ready. This gives the pup a big reward for coming when he is called.

CHILD'S PLAY

If you have children, you can make a game out of recall training.

- Make sure each child has some treats, and sit them in a circle or opposite each other.
- Each child, in turn, calls the puppy, using his name and the command "Come". When the pup comes, he is praised and given a treat before the next child calls him.
- As the pup progresses in his training, he can be asked to "Sit" before he is given his reward.

INTRODUCING DISTRACTIONS

As your puppy progresses with his recall training, you can step up the challenge by introducing distractions.

- Take your puppy out into the garden, and, when he is busy investigating an interesting smell, use his name and give the command "Come".
- Make sure you sound bright and exciting, so that your pup wants to come to you. When you have got his attention, crouch down, holding your arms out wide, making yourself appear as welcoming as possible.
- When your pup comes to you, even if his response has been slower than you would like, give lavish praise and reward him with a treat.
- Repeat the exercise on a regular basis, making it a fun part of your training sessions.
- At this stage, do not worry about asking the pup to Sit when he comes to you. You are trying to build up a fast, enthusiastic response – you can fine-tune it later when your puppy is ready to be taught a formal recall (see page 95).

EXTRA HELP

If your puppy is failing to respond, or is coming in at a snail's pace, you will need to recruit a helper to hold on to the pup.

- Show the puppy you have a treat, and then run off in the opposite direction.
- Call the puppy in an exciting voice. The moment you call, the helper should release the puppy.
- The pup should now have sufficient stimulation to respond. You can encourage him further by jumping up and down or running a few steps further. It does not matter how silly you look – it will be worth it when your pup comes running in. Give lots of praise, and reward.
- After a few sessions, your pup will catch on, and you can cut down on the theatricals!

NEW HORIZONS

The greatest challenge comes when your puppy has completed his vaccination course and can be taken to the local park, woods, or a field where he is allowed off the lead. Although you are asking a lot from your puppy, do not delay too long before taking this step. It is better to allow a puppy off-lead when he still feels vulnerable, as he will be anxious to stick close to you and will respond to being called. If you wait until your pup has grown into a boisterous adolescent, he will have become so frustrated that the first taste of freedom will probably go to his head, and you may struggle to get him back.

Introduce distractions by calling your pup away from a playmate.

To ensure success when you first attempt a recall away from home, try the following exercise:

• Recruit a helper and go to the park equipped with lots of treats and a training line. The training line should be made of rope and be approximately nine feet in length.
• Find an open space and attach the training line to the puppy's collar.
• Ask the helper to hold on to the puppy while you run off in the opposite direction, as you did in your early training.
• When the pup responds, he will come to you with the training line trailing. Lavish praise, and reward.
• If your pup gets distracted and tries to run off, your helper can stop him instantly by putting a foot on the line.

In most cases, the training line will prove to be an unnecessary precaution, but it will give you extra confidence. If your pup does attempt to take off, he will quickly learn that, somehow, you still retain control!

When you are ready, try a recall without the training line:

• Allow the pup to roam off-lead, and, after a few minutes, call him back. It is a good idea to time this when your pup is fairly close at hand so he is more likely to respond.
• When he comes to you, give lots of praise, and reward. Then continue with your walk.
• Repeat this exercise a few times as you walk. You want to reinforce the message that your pup comes and is rewarded, and then is allowed to go free again. Make sure you do not keep nagging at

SEEKING OUT

TRAINING TIP

To sharpen up your puppy's recall, recruit a helper to accompany you on a walk. At some point on the walk, ask the helper to hold on to your pup while you run out of sight, hiding behind a nearby tree or hedge. Call your pup, and he can seek you out. Make sure you give him lots of praise when he finds you.

Maximum distraction: The handler runs away while the dog is held by a helper. There are dogs on either side.

The dog's name is called, and he is released.

Ignoring all distractions, the dog heads for his handler.

The dog finds his handler behind a tree.

your pup, recalling him every few minutes, or he will soon lose interest in you.

- At the end of the walk, call your pup, reward him, and then have a quick game before snapping on the lead. In this way, he will not associate coming to you as signalling the end of his fun.

GOLDEN RULES

If you work hard in the early stages, your dog should soon build up a strong and reliable recall. To ensure continued success, keep to the following rules:

- Always reward your dog when he returns to you. If you do not have a treat, make sure you give him lots of fuss and praise.
- Never punish your dog when he comes to you, even though he may have taken his time and you are feeling extremely cross! The dog will not understand that he is being punished for being reluctant to come – he will think that coming to you means a telling off and no treats, so he won't bother responding next time.
- Call your dog when he is most likely to come. If you see him racing off with another dog, the chances of him coming back the second you give the command are slim – particularly while he is still young. Wait until you are close enough so that the pup can see his reward, and then call him. You may have to work hard, but your chances of success are greatly improved.
- Call your dog several times during the course of a walk. This helps you to maintain control, and it also means that the dog is not called only when the walk is at an end.

BEWARE!

It is great to get to the stage where you can allow your puppy free-running exercise, confident that he will return to you when called. However, do not make the mistake of allowing your pup unlimited exercise so that he comes back exhausted. You may think you are buying yourself some peace and quiet,

but you could be storing up serious trouble.

While your pup is growing, he risks serious injury if he over-exercises. This could take the form of osteochondrosis (or osteochondritis dissecans – OCD), a condition where cartilage fails to develop into bone. It most commonly affects the shoulder and elbow joints, and sometimes the stifle (hindleg joint corresponding to the dog's knee) and hocks (hindleg joint corresponding to the dog's ankle).

Hip dysplasia, a degenerative condition resulting from abnormal development of the hip joints, is exacerbated by over-exercise and putting too much strain on the developing joints.

TRAINING CLASSES

You and your puppy will both benefit from joining a training club. This provides the opportunity for you to be given help and guidance, and for your pup to meet other dogs. He will also learn to work in an environment that is full of distractions.

Some clubs allow you to join when your pup has received his first vaccination; others stipulate that the full vaccination course must be completed. Take time to find out about the clubs in your area so that you can find one that meets your needs. If your puppy's breeder lives locally, he or she may be able to recommend a suitable club, or you may have doggie friends who are members of a club.

Do not make the mistake of allowing a growing dog too much free-running exercise.

Otherwise, ask for details of local clubs at the veterinary practice.

Contact the club, and then go along to a class without your puppy. Check out the following:

- **Does the club use reward-based training?** You do not want to have anything to do with instructors that rely on punitive techniques.
- **Do any of the instructors have experience with your breed of dog?** This is not essential, but it is certainly helpful if the instructor understands the typical mind-set, rate of learning, and capabilities of your breed.
- **Are the classes divided according to age and experience of the dogs?** This is not always possible if the club is very small, but it is certainly desirable. It means that young pups are not frightened by bigger dogs, and the exercises will be of a suitable standard.
- **Does the club run the Good Citizen Award Scheme?** This is a scheme devised by the Kennel Club to promote responsible ownership and to produce model canine citizens. Most of the exercises that are included are covered in this chapter (including handling and grooming), and they provide a very sound foundation for a puppy's education. Guide Dog puppy walkers are encouraged to take the awards, which graduate from bronze to silver, and then on to gold.

If you are happy with what you see at the training club, you can make arrangements to join. If you do not think it is well run, look elsewhere. It may mean that you have to travel a little further, but it is well worth it to find the best possible club.

ADVANCED EXERCISES

When your puppy has mastered the basic exercises, you may want to try some more advanced training. There is no set age when a puppy is ready to take on new challenges. Every dog is an individual and the skill of the trainer is to move at a pace that suits a particular dog.

If you enrol at a training club, you will get help

Your pup will benefit from attending a training class, as long as it is well run and focuses on reward-based methods.

and guidance with more advanced training, but the following exercises will give you an idea of how to expand your dog's education.

FORMAL RECALL

If your puppy comes when he is called, you may be content to rest on your laurels. However, if you want to take training a step further, or you are interested in Competitive Obedience (see page 126), you may want to teach a formal recall.

This is a useful exercise, as it strings a number of components together. An intelligent dog will enjoy the stimulation of learning a more complex lesson, and it will raise his level of response and obedience.

The aim is to build up a really enthusiastic response to the recall.

- Start with the puppy on your left-hand side, and ask him to "Sit".
- Command "Wait", and leave your dog, stepping off with your right foot (a dog is less likely to follow if you step off on the foot furthest from him). In the early stages of training, you may need to repeat the "Wait" command as you walk away.
- Walk a distance away, halt, turn, and face your pup. If the puppy looks unsteady, as if he is about to break position, repeat "Wait".
- Place your feet slightly apart, so that your pup has a place to aim for, and then call him: "Sammy, Come".
- As your pup comes in front of you, give the command "Sit". You can end the exercise here, giving lots of praise and a reward. In Competitive Obedience, the dog must "Finish" by returning to the heel position.

INSTANT DOWN

This is a more advanced form of training, but it is worth working at, as it gives you instant control when the dog is off-lead. It is useful in a variety of situations, and it could turn out to be a lifesaver in an emergency. There are two methods of teaching the Emergency Down.

METHOD ONE

Wait until your pup is walking confidently on a lead and is responding consistently to the "Down" before teaching this exercise.

- Start by walking with your dog on a loose lead, halt, and give the command "Down".
- You will have taken your dog by surprise, so you may need to crouch down by his side and use your hand to lure him to the ground, as you did in his early training.
- Keep your dog in the "Down" for a few moments, praise and reward, and then continue walking.
- Repeat this exercise until your pup is responding to the verbal command and does not need additional aids.
- Now step up a gear, and try the same exercise with the dog running beside you. Initially, you may have more control if the dog is on-lead.
- Give a short, sharp command to encourage an instant response. When your dog responds, give lots of praise and reward, and then pick up the pace again.
- In time, your pup will learn to respond instantly, wait for the release command, and then be ready to run with you again.

METHOD TWO

Do not teach this method until your dog responds to the "Wait" command and has a strong recall. It is particularly important not to train this too early, or it could have a detrimental effect on your dog's recall.

- Command "Sit" and "Wait", and leave your dog.
- Walk a distance away, then turn and face your dog.

An instant response to the Down could be a lifesaver.

- Give the command "Come", but keep the command low-key so that your dog does not set off with an explosive burst of speed.
- If he is coming in too fast, give a command such as "Steady" so that the dog is listening to you, waiting for the next command.
- When your dog is halfway towards you, give the command "Down". It may help if you position a mat so the dog has a specific place to aim for.
- Your dog may be slow to go into position, so you may need to repeat the command in a deep, firm voice. Praise him quietly when he goes into the correct position.
- Wait a few moments and then call the dog to you. He deserves lots of praise and a big treat for completing this exercise.
- Keep practising, and soon your pup will understand what is required and will go into the Down instantly.

RETRIEVE

This is a fun exercise, which helps to build up a good relationship between you and your dog. Many well-trained guide dogs enjoy a game of retrieve, bringing a ball or toy back to their owner. It also provides an excellent opportunity for controlled, free-running exercise.

You can train the retrieve as a formal exercise, or you may wish to keep it as a game. In both situations, make sure you control proceedings, and if your dog has a slightly obsessive nature, make sure he does not become too ball- or toy-orientated.

- Find a toy that your puppy really likes, and keep this as his 'retrieve' toy. Start by encouraging the pup to play with the toy so that he gets really keen on it.
- Throw the toy a few feet away, and your pup should run after it. As he runs out, give the command "Fetch".
- If your puppy is slow to catch on, you will need to work harder at getting him interested in the toy – hiding it behind your back, throwing it up in the air… anything that makes the pup keen to get hold of it.
- When the pup picks up the toy, give the command "Hold", and then call the pup to you. This is often the hardest bit, as the pup may be keen to run off with his trophy.
- The best plan is to have a toy at the ready so you can encourage your pup to come to you and then swap toys with him. When the pup gives up his toy, use the command "Give".
- Now throw his retrieve toy again, and repeat the exercise. If you keep practising, the pup will learn that, if he brings the toy back, you will throw it for him, thus continuing the game.

> **TRAINING TIP**
>
> If your pup is determined to run off with his toy, try tying it to a length of string. Throw the toy, and when your pup runs out to get it, you can still keep control of it. Give a gentle tug on the string and call the puppy to you, guiding him to bring the toy back.

Once your dog has mastered a play retrieve, you can progress to the formal exercise.

1. Start by asking the dog to sit at your left-hand side.

2. He must wait while the dumb-bell is thrown.

3. The handler gives the command to "Fetch".

FORMAL RETRIEVE

Once your pup has mastered the retrieve, you may want to make it into a formal exercise. There are a number of elements to string together, and it will take some time before your puppy can complete the full exercise.

- Ask your puppy to "Sit" at your left-hand side. Throw the toy (or dumb-bell), and tell him to "Wait".
- Send the puppy to retrieve the toy, using the command "Fetch".
- As he picks up the dumb-bell, say "Hold", and then call the pup to you.
- The dog should come in straight and sit in front of you to present the toy.
- Command "Give" so that the pup releases the toy to your hand. If you want, give the command "Finish" so that the pup returns to the heel position.

SENDAWAY

This exercise involves the dog being sent away from the handler, running to a designated spot and going into the Down. It is one of the more difficult exercises to teach, as most training involves the dog coming to you rather than encouraging him to work independently.

Start by teaching the "Away" command, which means the pup must run away from you to a specific spot. You can make this as easy as possible.

- When your pup is due to be fed, hold on to him while a helper places his food bowl at the far end of the kitchen. Give the command "Away" and your pup will run out to get to his food bowl.
- Take your pup to his bed or his indoor kennel, and stand a short distance from it. Give the command "Away", and the pup will head for his bed/indoor kennel.
- Some breeds, such as Golden Retrievers, love car

travel, and cannot wait to leap into the back of the vehicle. Assuming your pup is old enough to jump into the car (see page 103), you can open the back of the vehicle, take the pup a distance from it, and then give the command "Away".

• When your pup has mastered "Away", you will need to work at the "Down", which is required when the pup reaches the designated spot.

• Use a mat, place a toy or a treat on it, then ask your pup to go into the "Down".

• Next place a toy or treat on the mat, and take the puppy from it. Give the command "Away", run

with your pup, and then command "Down" as soon as he reaches the mat.

• When the pup realises that a toy/treat is on the mat, he should respond to the "Away" command without assistance. Give the "Down" command as soon as he reaches the mat.

• If you practise regularly, your pup will soon learn to go into the Down as soon as he reaches the mat. Eventually, he will be able to do the exercise without a toy or treat on the mat, and he will wait until the exercise is over before he is rewarded.

The dog must learn to run out to an allocated spot and go into the Down.

CHAPTER SEVEN

PUPPY SOCIALISATION

Without doubt, the most important part of training a puppy is undertaking a comprehensive programme of socialisation. Obviously, you want to work at basic obedience exercises, but the timing of this type of training is not crucial. When it comes to socialising a puppy – getting him used to the sights and sounds of everyday life – time is of the essence.

A puppy will soak up new experiences like a sponge, and the more you can do with a youngster in the first 12 months, the more well balanced and adaptable the dog will be as an adult. When a puppy is socialised at this impressionable time of his life, he may come across situations that he initially dislikes, or even fears. But, with the right handling, the pup has the capacity to learn that there is nothing to be concerned about, and he will get over his reservations. This is in marked contrast to an adult who has not been properly socialised. This type of dog will form an impression – good or bad – and stick with it. It takes a tremendous amount of time and patience to work with an adult who has developed phobias due to lack of early socialisation.

It is no different to keeping a child confined at home, and allowing that child to grow up without seeing anything of the outside world. When that individual is eventually taken to a busy area to see real life for the first time, it is no surprise that he cannot cope.

A puppy should be exposed to as many different experiences as possible during his formative months.

Do not go out of your way to find something to 'spook' your puppy – even the soundest animal will have some concerns. Equally, do not drown your puppy with so much stimulation that he starts to dread going out! Find a balance, making use of everyday opportunities to educate your puppy. Your job is to introduce him to the outside world in a calm, relaxed manner, giving him the confidence to take life in his stride.

A puppy will soak up new experiences like a sponge.

Sit on a bench and let your pup watch the world go by from the safety of your lap.

FIRST STEPS

If your vet has agreed to start your puppy's vaccination programme at six to eight weeks, you will be able to take your puppy out and about almost as soon as he arrives in his new home. Obviously, you will need to take certain precautions to ensure the pup is not exposed to areas that are heavily used by other dogs (see page 48).

If vaccinations are delayed for several weeks, you will have to be more cautious. You want to protect your puppy from all risk of infection, but, equally, you do not want to lose valuable socialising time by keeping him confined to the house and garden. In fact, you can overcome this problem quite easily by letting the pup see the outside world from the security of your arms.

You do not have to carry the pup for miles! Go to a busy area and find a bench where you can sit with the puppy on your lap. The pup has the chance to get used to the sound of traffic, and he can watch all the comings and goings while feeling safe in your arms. Few people can resist a puppy, and you will almost certainly find yourself the centre of attention as people come up to say hello to the pup. This is excellent for the puppy's development, as he will get used to being petted by strangers, and will learn that people do not constitute a threat.

CAR TRAVEL

Socialising your pup in these early weeks will be much easier if you can take him to different places in the car. Indeed, learning to travel in a car is all part of his education.

The safest place for a dog to travel is in the rear of the car, preferably confined in an indoor kennel, or restricted to his area by a dog-guard. Your puppy will be happy with this arrangement once he understands that the area you have allocated is his place, and he is not allowed to go anywhere else in the car. Most dogs love car travel, but you may have a few noisy journeys while your puppy gets used to the new experience. Observe the following rules, and your pup should soon become a contented passenger.

- Never feed your puppy before a journey.
- Make the indoor kennel/dog space comfortable, lining it with bedding. Some puppies settle better if you provide a toy to chew on.
- Settle your pup in his allocated space, and then go on a short trip.

- If the pup protests, ignore him. There is no point in trying to make yourself heard above his din, and your added noise will only make the puppy more hyped up.
- When you reach your destination, do not rush round to release your pup. Wait until he is quiet, tell him to "Wait", and then open the door. Clip on his lead, and then lift him out of the car.
- It is essential to observe this car drill every time you take the puppy out of the car. It will teach him not to come flying out, which could have fatal consequences.

GROWING PAINS

To begin with, your pup will be too small to jump in and out of the car. But if you have a medium to large breed, it will not be long before your pup thinks he is ready to manage the car on his own. However, it is vital that you continue lifting the pup in and out of the car while he is young and the bone structure is developing. The joints of a growing puppy are very vulnerable, and they should not be subjected to undue strain.

> **TRAINING TIP**
> If your pup is failing to settle in the car, or if he is suffering from car-sickness, make sure every car trip ends on a treat. Visit a friend who has a dog that your puppy likes to play with, or, once he has completed his vaccinations, take him to the park. In this way, the puppy will build up good associations with the car, and will learn to settle.

CAR-SICKNESS

Some puppies suffer from car-sickness, or they may drool excessively.

In most cases, a puppy will grow out of this problem once he is used to the motion of the car. It is important to continue taking the pup out, even if he is car-sick. If you wait for a few weeks, the puppy will have a bad association with the car, and the problem will probably get worse.

If you are concerned that your pup is not overcoming his car-sickness within a few weeks, you can ask your vet to prescribe some suitable tablets.

If your pup learns to travel quietly, he will be included in all the family's excursions.

Now is the time to put your puppy's lead training into practice!

As your puppy increases in confidence, try out more challenging environments.

PUPPY PARTIES

Many veterinary practices organise puppy parties, which provide an ideal opportunity for socialising. In most cases, they are open to pups after they have received their first vaccination.

The advantage of these groups is that the puppies are all roughly the same age, and so there is no danger of a pup being frightened by a bigger, more boisterous animal.

The pups play together in a controlled situation so they learn how to respond to each other. This continues the lessons the puppies learnt when they were playing with their siblings. Canine communication – understanding another dog's intentions from his demeanour and from his body language – is all part of the learning process.

The puppies will also meets lots of new people, which will help to boost confidence.

VET VISIT

Guide Dog puppy walkers are encouraged to visit the veterinarian's surgery on a routine basis so that the pup becomes accustomed to the place and does not associate it with anything unpleasant. This saves a lot of problems later in the pup'slife. For example, you could take your pup to be weighed, or bring him with you when you go to collect worming or flea treatments.

RARING TO GO

When your puppy has completed his vaccinations, socialisation can begin in earnest. Hopefully, you will have worked on lead-training (see page 84), and your pup will be ready to walk with you in a relatively civilised manner.

To begin with, choose a fairly quiet area, such as a housing estate, where there is not too much traffic. You can practise walking to heel in a different environment where distractions are not too daunting.

• Adopt a bright and breezy manner, and set off at a good pace. You want your pup to step out confidently, so do not nag him if he is a little

Meeting another dog will teach good manners.

forward in his position.
- If the pup gets carried away and starts pulling on the lead, stop and call him back to your side before setting off again.
- If the pup lags behind, or becomes distracted by interesting smells, use your voice, and a treat if necessary, to encourage him to walk with you. Sniffing on the lead is a bad habit in all dogs, and is a very serious fault in guide dog puppies, so it should be corrected immediately.
- Use treats intermittently, so that your pup does not become obsessed by them but so that you have some ammunition if you are experiencing problems.

STEPPING UP A GEAR
When your puppy is walking quietly in a residential area, you can step up the pace and move on to a more challenging environment. Do not be in a hurry to do this if your pup is showing concern over traffic. Some breeds, and indeed some individuals, are more sound sensitive than others, so you need to monitor your puppy's reactions. If he is steaming along, without a care in the world, he is ready to move on. If he is showing traffic awareness, keep to the quiet areas and give the pup a little longer to become accustomed to noise levels.

- When you start working in a busier environment, you will have to work harder at keeping your puppy's attention.
- Keep talking to the pup, encouraging him to walk with you in a bright, confident manner.
- If your pup sees or hears something unfamiliar, he may well stop to find out what is going on. This is okay in the early stages of training. Give the pup a chance to evaluate what he has seen or heard, and then encourage him to walk on with you. As the pup becomes more experienced, the number of stop-starts will decrease, and will eventually disappear.
- If your pup is frightened by something, he may dig in his heels and refuse to walk past. Be 'matter of fact' about the incident, and do not make an issue of it. Confidence will transmit from you to the pup. It is often better to shrug your shoulders, walk off somewhere else, and then return as though nothing had happened.
- Can you use treats in these situations? Yes! There is absolutely no logical reason for not using anything that quickly and effortlessly helps you and your pup to overcome a problem. Once the pup is happy to, for example, go up and down a metal fire escape following a few favourite treats, then there should be no need to keep giving them.

While your pup is learning, you should expose him to as many different situations as possible. Go looking for places that may be familiar to you, but that will be strange, and possibly worrying, for a young puppy. The more work you put in now, the more adaptable your dog will be in his adult life. Even if he encounters a new situation, a well-socialised dog will have the confidence to approach without fear.

A dog is only allowed into a shop, a café or a restaurant at the discretion of those who run the business. Nearly all such places welcome guide dogs, and many will also allow guide dog puppies. A pet dog is more restricted in places to go, but if you use your imagination, you can still give your pup a well-rounded education.

- Go to a shopping centre and walk among the crowds. Although you cannot go into food stores, you will be allowed to enter some shops that are not so dog-sensitive – banks and post offices are usually okay. This type of establishment often has a slippery floor, which will be a new experience. If you hunt around, you can also find a variety of doors: swing doors, revolving doors, and doors that open and shut automatically. These all provide learning opportunities.

- Go to a big car park (a supermarket car park is ideal) and take your pup for a walk. There will be cars pulling in and out of parking bays, people pushing trolleys, and very often the crash of bottles at the recycling unit. This is also a good opportunity to practise some basic exercises, such as Sit and Down, so that the pup gets used to listening to you and doing as he is asked in a different environment.

A trip to a shopping centre provides a wealth of new experiences.

Have a walk round the supermarket car park – there's always plenty going on.

- A busy market is an excellent place to take your puppy. The aisles are usually narrow and crowded with people, the stalls have music blaring out, and there are rows of clothes flapping in the wind. Best of all, the ground is littered with squashed chips and other delicacies. You will have your work cut out to keep your puppy walking with you in this situation, but take your time and have lots of encouragement as you work your way through the crowds.

- Visit the local primary school when it is home-time. The road will be full of parked cars, there will be mums and dads with toddlers and pushchairs – and loads of school-age children all keen to stroke your puppy. If you do not have children in your family, this is a particularly good option to choose as a socialising situation.

Let your pup meet groups of children.

If you go to the park, you can be certain that your pup will attract attention.

- There is often a football match going on at the local park at weekends. This time, make sure your pup is on the lead, and go and stand at the touchline with your pup sitting beside you. The pup will learn that, even though he can see people running and shouting, he must remain quiet and calm.

- Go to the local park, and if your pup is reliable on the recall, allow him to have some free-running exercise. He will probably meet some dogs, as well as other people who are out walking. If the puppy has an opportunity to socialise off-lead, he will become more confident, rather than always relying on you.

- Most parks have a play area, and even though dogs are not allowed in this part, you can go and sit on a nearby bench. Your puppy will see children running, and shouting – sometimes screaming with excitement. If he sits quietly next to you, watching, he will get used to the noise, and it will not trigger a reaction.

- Railway stations are really good for finding new experiences. The fact that you may never use trains is not the point of the exercise. Look for escalators, lifts, or fire escapes, let him see trains and even get on and off one. Unusual noises, fumes and sudden movements can initially worry him, but when he shows concern, try to be confident yourself.

The railway station is full of different sights and sounds.

Try taking your pup for a journey on the train.

TRAINING TIP

A pup can learn unconsciously, and this is a good tool to use in certain situations. If your pup has shown some concern over unusual noises, go to a railway station or a bus station armed with the pup's favourite treats.

Just as the train draws into the station, or the bus pulls away, produce the treats. The pup will be so delighted with the surprise reward, he will not pay attention to what is going on around him. Try this on a few occasions, and the pup will unconsciously become accustomed to the noise level, and it will cease to worry him.

- A building site or a place where road works are being carried out is a challenge for your pup as he grows in confidence. The noise from the machinery can be horrendous, so do not plunge into this situation until you feel your puppy is able to cope.

- If you live in the town, your pup is unlikely to come across sheep, cows, horses, poultry, and other farm animals. It is important that a pup learns that these animals are off-limits, so make sure you find a socialising situation – even if it means taking your pup for a day out in the country. If there is an agricultural show or country fair being held in your area, this will provide an opportunity to encounter livestock, farm machinery, and crowds all in one go!

- Puppy socialisation is not always hard work. If you have a local pub that welcomes dogs, do take advantage. Pubs are excellent for socialising pups as well as humans! There are always customers who wish to meet and make a fuss of a young pup. This, coupled with the sound of the jukebox, gaming machines and mobile phones going off, provide an excellent introduction to life. In time, you can encourage your puppy to lie down close to the bar where he will get used to people leaning over the top of him while their pints are being replenished. There are 'No dogs' restrictions in some pubs that have dining facilities, but you can still find some that will allow dogs.

TRAINING TIPS

- *If your pup shows undue interest in an animal, distract his attention with a treat, and then reward him. Next time he looks at the animal, use the command "Leave", and reward him as soon as he looks away. In this way, the pup learns he is under your control, and must behave in an appropriate manner when other animals are around.*

- *If your pup seems particularly focused on livestock, you may have to seek out situations on a regular basis to work on this aspect of his behaviour.*

- *If you are working in a challenging environment, it can help if you meet up with a friend who has an older dog who is calm and confident in all situations. If you walk together, the puppy will learn from the older dog, and will realise that there is nothing to fear.*

Find a way of letting your pup see different sorts of livestock.

Norma Stent is currently one of Guide Dogs' longest serving puppy walkers. She had her first puppy in 1980, and she has walked a pup every year since then. At the moment, she is walking Candy, a seven-month-old Labrador-Curly Coat cross.

"I first heard about puppy walking when I was expecting my first child," said Norma. "I was worried about taking on a 12- to 14-year commitment for a dog, and I thought puppy walking seemed an ideal solution. You could take on a puppy for a year, but if you wanted to give up after that, it was no problem. We took on out first puppy, and then we got hooked on it!"

Now Norma's children have grown up and left home, but the puppies keep on coming. She has puppy walked a wide variety of breeds including Labradors, Labrador-Retriever crosses, Golden Retrievers, Border Collies, German Shepherds, a Collie-Retriever cross, and a Flat Coat-Retriever cross.

"I have loved them all," said Norma. "They have all been so different, and I look on every puppy as a new challenge. You get something out of every dog you walk, but there are some that you find it easier to relate to."

Guide dog puppy Candy.

Her most recent favourite was Arnie, a Flat Coat-Retriever cross.

"He was drop dead gorgeous. He was a really wonderful dog. There was only one pup I struggled with, and that was a German Shepherd who had very dominant tendencies. In fact, she settled down after her first season and became a pleasure to live with."

Norma calculates her success rate of puppies that have gone on to qualify as guide dogs is around 70 per cent.

Guide dog puppy Arnie (second left with his siblings).

"A few dogs were rejected on health grounds, and some have been chosen as breeding stock, which makes me very proud. But when it comes down to it, you have to work with the puppy you have been given, and make the best of it."

Norma gives talks for Guide Dogs, and she is also a regular speaker at schools and colleges, as well as being an ardent fundraiser.

"Wherever I go, the guide dog puppy comes too. It really is a case of 'love me, love my dog.' If I go to the doctor, the dentist, or the hairdresser, the puppy comes too. I take the pup into shops, restaurants, and cafés. In fact, 99 per cent of the time, the puppy simply accompanies me in my usual routine. The only time I make special trips to socialise the puppy is when I use public transport. We get so used to using the car all the time that I have to make a conscious effort to go on a bus or a train.

"At our local railway station they know me so well that I can ask when a train is due to arrive and find out how long it will be in the station. Then I get on the train with the pup and walk from one end to the other before it is due to depart. This gives the puppy the experience of getting on and off the train, he hears all the noise, and feels the vibration of the train."

Guide Dog puppy Gemma.

Norma's husband, Derek, is also involved with training the puppies.

"Derek like the pups when they first arrive, and I get more involved when they are around 5-6 months, so it works well."

Do they plan to carry on puppy walking?

"Oh, yes," said Norma with out hesitation.""We wouldn't like an empty house. There are times in the depths of winter when you have to go out in the garden for the pup to empty, and you think: 'Why am I doing this?' – but the feeling doesn't last for long!"

Guide Dog puppy Eve.

Guide Dog puppy George.

CHAPTER EIGHT

GROWING UP

When you are rearing a puppy, there is often a honeymoon period when everything seems to be going right. You have overcome all the 'little puppy' problems of house-training and chewing, and the pup has settled into your home and become part of the family. He has mastered the basic training exercises, and is a pleasure to take out.

For a brief period, you think you have cracked it – and then everything changes with the onset of adolescence. The puppy who was obedient and eager to please suddenly 'forgets' his lessons; the well-balanced, adaptable youngster develops phobias overnight, and you are left wondering what you have done wrong.

THE ADOLESCENT DOG

The age at which a dog hits adolescence varies from breed to breed. The smaller Toy dogs will often mature earlier and may show adolescent behaviour from six months onwards. The bigger breeds will show marked behavioural changes from around nine months. The changes coincide with the dog's sexual maturity and the increase of hormonal activity. This is often more noticeable in males, but a female awaiting the start of her first season can cause her fair share of problems too.

Some dogs sail through adolescence, moving effortlessly from puppyhood to adulthood. However, the majority, like human teenagers, find life difficult for a short period.

WHAT IS GOING ON?

If you have established yourself as a firm, fair and consistent leader, your pup will have accepted his place in the human pack. However, as the hormones start pumping round his body, he will start to question the status quo. In the wild, adolescent youngsters in a wolf pack re-negotiate their ranking as they mature, and the biggest, boldest animals may even mount a challenge for leadership.

The adolescent dog starts to test the boundaries that have been imposed upon him.

The domesticated dog is following exactly the same pattern of behaviour. Instead of seeking the protection of the pack and the pack leader, he is aware of his growing strength and sexuality, and he feels he should better his position.

WHAT SHOULD YOU DO?

Do not despair! This is only a passing phase, and if you handle your dog with a mixture of firmness and sensitivity, you will soon win back the dog that is a pleasure to own. Puppy walkers who take on a pup every year are all too familiar with adolescent agonies. But equally, they have seen it all before, and know that there is light at the end of the tunnel.

When dealing with an adolescent dog – male or female – bear in mind the following points:

• Give your dog plenty of mental stimulation. If his mind is occupied, he will have less energy for dreaming up his own agenda.
• Work at all the basic training exercises. This will underline your position as leader, and your dog will benefit from the positive interaction.
• If your dog 'forgets' his lessons – for example, if he starts to ignore the recall command – go back to basics. Start training as if your adolescent youngster was a small puppy. This will sharpen up his responses, and will give you the opportunity to praise good behaviour rather than constantly nagging him for disobeying.
• Set up for success, and only give commands when they are most likely to be obeyed. This is not 'giving in' to bad behaviour. It is a matter of working with the positives so that the dog accepts your authority rather than getting into the habit of ignoring your commands.
• Be lavish in your use of rewards so that your dog is motivated to do as you ask. Now is the time to use his favourite food treats, or to have lots of play sessions with his special toy.
• Make sure you and your family are consistent in enforcing all the house rules. Your dog is likely to push his luck; he may suddenly decide he should sleep on the sofa or raid the bin, so you must be quick to put him back in his place.

Make sure you are consistent in your training.

DEVELOPING PHOBIAS

One of the most frustrating aspects of adolescent behaviour is the dog that suddenly develops phobias. A pup that has been well socialised will be taking most situations in his stride, and you will be happy with his progress. Then, out of nowhere, the pup decides he is frightened of a bin bag left in the street, or a man carrying an umbrella. The dog may have passed these 'hazards' hundreds of times before, but, for no apparent reason, he takes a dislike to them.

Work through this phase in exactly the way you did when first socialising your puppy. Adopt a no-nonsense manner, and encourage your dog to walk with you. You may find it useful to have a supply of your dog's favourite treats to use in these situations.

Do not make a big issue of the phobia, or your dog will start to take himself seriously! In time, he will grow out of this phase, and will forget his temporary neurosis.

CANINE RELATIONS

As your pup matures, he will reassess his relationships with other dogs. He is no longer the sweet pup who submits to every adult he meets. He is now ready (or almost ready) to relate on an equal footing.

If you have a resident dog, you may find that relations become a little strained as the adolescent becomes more assertive. You may find that the resident dog retains superiority, and the youngster settles down and accepts his lower ranking. Alternatively, the younger dog may become the boss. This is very much a matter that the two dogs will sort out for themselves, and you should not attempt to intervene.

Once the issue has been sorted out, you should go with the flow and support the higher-ranking dog's authority when you are interacting with the two dogs.

For example, feed the higher-ranking dog first, put his lead on first when you are going out for a walk, or get him out of the car first. This will ensure that the dogs live together in harmony, with no need to fight over status.

During this time, restrict interactions with other dogs to tried-and-trusted individuals who will not take any nonsense from an adolescent youngster. It is far better if an adult of sound temperament gives an occasional warning growl when a youngster steps out of line, rather than exposing your pup to a scrap in the park with the local canine thug!

Relations between dogs may change as the youngster grows up.

There are many health benefits associated with neutering.

NEUTERING

Unless a dog is to be selected for breeding stock, all Guide Dog puppies are neutered. This is an obvious necessity for a working dog, but it makes complete sense for all animals who are not going to be used for breeding.

There are health and behavioural benefits associated with neutering both males and females, and it also makes life easier for the owner.

FEMALES

- The spayed female will not come into season every nine months or so. This eliminates the need to keep her isolated from males during the 21-day cycle.
- There is no chance of false pregnancies, which can occur after a bitch has been in season.
- The neutered bitch does not run the risk of developing pyometra (a potentially life-threatening condition where the womb fills with pus).
- The chances of developing mammary cancer are minimised.

MALES

- A castrated male will not be preoccupied with looking for females in season.
- Scent marking (when the male cocks his leg and leaves a few drops of urine to mark his territory) is minimised.
- Aggressive behaviour towards other dogs is reduced.
- The risk of testicular cancer is eliminated.
- The chance of developing prostate disorders is reduced.

GETTING THE TIMING RIGHT

The health benefits of neutering will kick in when the surgery is carried out, regardless of the age of the dog. However, if you are seeking to influence behaviour, it is essential to get the timing absolutely right – particularly when dealing with castration.

A number of organisations that work with rescued dogs have a policy of neutering young – often when the dog is less than six months of age. The main reason for this is to ensure the dog is neutered before it is rehomed. If you do not have these considerations, you can be more flexible, waiting for the most appropriate time.

It is generally recommended that females are spayed after they have had their first season, and at the mid-point before their next season is due. At this stage, the female has reached full physical maturity, which is the optimum moment for carrying out the operation. Guide dog bitches will usually have the operation before leaving the puppy walker's home, as it has been found that bitches recover far more quickly when they are in a familiar place.

It is more difficult to be specific about the timing of castration in males. Again, it is generally advisable to wait until the dog has reached full physical maturity before operating, but it is as important not to delay too long. If a male is dominant and is behaving aggressively or assertively, you cannot rely on castration to solve his behavioural problems. He has already learnt to behave in a particular manner, and it will be difficult to change his mind set.

At Guide Dogs, the majority of males will be castrated at around nine months of age. If a male is becoming over-assertive, an early castration will be planned. Equally, if a male is lacking in boldness, and is clearly immature for his age, the operation will be delayed for a month or so.

If you are planning to neuter your dog, monitor his behaviour to work out the optimum time for castration. If in doubt, consult your vet.

WHEN THINGS GO WRONG

Despite all your best efforts, there are times when training breaks down. This can be blamed on adolescence, or you may have allowed bad habits to develop. The most important point to bear in mind is that nearly all problems are solvable – even though it may take time and patience. You need to be prepared to identify the problem, work out what is going on, and then find a solution. Do not give up, resigning yourself to undesirable behaviour. In no time, the dog will be ruling the roost, and you will find yourself repeatedly giving in to his demands.

Trainee guide dogs have the best possible start in life, in terms of breeding, rearing and training, but problems can still occur. This is particularly the case when a sensitive dog has to change allegiance, going from puppy walker to trainer, and then to his blind owner. If a dog comes under pressure, he may revert to a form of undesirable behaviour, as he has no other way to express his feelings.

In nearly all cases, these problems can be worked through, and the dog will rediscover his equilibrium.

DOMINANCE ISSUES

If you have worked hard at training, and have established a good relationship with your dog,

dominance issues are unlikely to occur. The adolescent dog may seek to challenge your authority, but if you are respected as the leader, and you underline your position by training and by increasing motivation, most dogs will quickly step back into line.

Problems with dominance generally arise because a dog has not been given firm leadership, and he has decided to make up his code of conduct. This type of behaviour can take a number of different forms:

BREAKING HOUSE RULES: The dog decides he has the right to sleep on the sofa, to beg at the table, or to jump up at you when you come in.

GENERAL DISOBEDIENCE: The dog takes his time when you ask him to do something, or he even ignores you altogether.

Despite your best efforts, training problems may arise as your dog reaches maturity.

Gill Chard has been a Guide Dog puppy walker for the past 16 years, and she has walked a puppy every year during that time. At the moment she is caring for Cathy, a yellow Labrador bitch.

"I have puppy walked Labradors, Golden Retrievers, Labrador-Retriever crosses, and a Flat Coat-Retriever cross, and I can quite honestly say that every dog has been different. Obviously, there are certain breed characteristics that you come to know, but I am far more aware of the fact that every dog is an individual.

"The Labrador-Retriever cross produces some good, sound dogs, and I enjoyed walking the Flat Coat-Retriever cross. She looked the image of a Flat Coat, but I think the Golden Retriever blood made her a little bit calmer.

"I was always told that males were harder to train than females, but that has not been my experience. In fact, the two dogs I would class as my favourites over the years were both Golden Retriever males. I have found some males to be quite challenging, but the females have thrown up different sorts of problems."

Gill is now a very experienced puppy walker, which she says helps her to spot signs of trouble at an early stage and to start dealing with them.

"In my early days, I had a Labrador male called York. He really was quite a challenge. When he became adolescent, he became quite bolshie and demanding. If I were washing up, he would suddenly jump up at me and start barking. He would never do it to John, my husband, but he thought he could try it on with me."

With the help of the puppy walking supervisor, Gill got to work on York.

"We needed to be very firm with him, and we used strong, assertive body language so that he understood who was in charge. We took certain steps to lower his status. For example, I would sit in his dog bed, and before I gave him his food, I would pretend to eat from his bowl. I was quite naive in those days, so I did find it difficult. But you have to learn to think like a dog so that you can see the world through his eyes. When it comes down to it, it is simply a matter of using your common sense."

York got over his dominance issues, and went on to qualify as a guide dog. Gill is now experiencing some adolescent agonies with her six-month-old bitch, Cathy.

"She has not yet had her first season, and her hormones are all over the place. She is very excitable, and she wants to jump up at people when we are out on walks. She has also started being worried by situations where she was previously okay. Today, I took her out, and we tried to go up some steps at the railway station. The steps are open and the situation is quite exposed, but that would not have worried her a couple of months ago.

"She made a big fuss, so I am going back with my husband tomorrow and we will set up a training

POSSESSIVENESS/ GUARDING: The dog becomes possessive about a particular toy, and growls if you try to take it away.

Your dog may become possessive about a variety of things, including his bed/indoor kennel, warning you off if you come too close. Or he may become possessive about his food, growling if you interfere with him while he is eating.

AGGRESSION: In some cases, the dog may become aggressive towards other dogs. In very rare cases, he may show aggression towards people. If the latter situation arises, you must seek immediate help from an experienced trainer or reputable behaviourist. A dog that is aggressive towards people could end up in serious trouble, and it is your responsibility to call in expert help without delay.

situation. Cassie likes us to walk together, so I will walk her on the lead, and my husband will go to the top of the stairs and call her. We will both have some treats, so we can reward her as she goes up the stairs, and when she gets to the top. If we work at it, she will be fine. It's just a temporary setback, which you really can blame on adolescence."

Gill has also found that some of her adolescent puppies have a 'wall of death' phase, when they career round and round a room at breakneck speed.

"It's a mixture of over-excitement and attention-seeking," said Gill. "If it happens, all I do is get hold of the pup, and put him or her out of the room for five minutes. The pup is completely ignored, so learns that the attention-seeking behaviour does not work. After five minutes, I allow the pup to come back into the room with us, and praise him or her for being calm and quiet."

Gill finds that the bitches calm down a lot after they have had their first season.

"I usually see the behaviour improving, but I rarely get the full benefit, as, by that time, the dog will be ready to go into training."

A large number of Gill's puppies have qualified as guide dogs, but inevitably there are those that do not make it.

"At the end of the day, you are given a dog to work with; sometimes you can overcome problems and sometimes you cannot. The dogs that have been rejected may be too distracted by other dogs, or they spend when they are out on a walk. These would be minor problems in a pet dog, but they are unacceptable in a guide dog."

Occasionally, Gill has been tempted to keep a dog that has not qualified, but she has decided to concentrate on puppy walking.

"Every dog throws up something different, and you are constantly working at different aspects of a puppy's training and behaviour. I find it challenging, but also very rewarding. There is no such thing as a totally perfect puppy – anyway I think it would be boring if all puppies were the same and you had nothing to work on and improve."

Guide Dog puppy Cathy: "Every puppy is a challenge."

ACTION PLAN

If you fear your dog is becoming too dominant, you need to lower his self-esteem so that he is prepared to accept your authority. This is vital if you are not to end up with a dog that completely ignores any command you direct at him. Depending on the type of dominant behaviour your dog is showing, this can be tackled on a number of fronts:

HOUSE RULES

Make sure you and your family are 100 per cent consistent in applying house rules. "Give him an inch and he takes a mile" is a great truism in this situation.

• If you see your dog on the sofa, he must be told to get off instantly. If he growls in protest, do not buy his act. You are setting the rules, not the dog.

- If your dog jumps up, firmly put all four paws on the ground. Do not speak to him until he is in the correct position – then you can praise him and tell him what a good dog he is.

TRAINING

- Work at training exercises, always giving yourself the best possible chance of success (see Chapter 6).
- Use every opportunity to lower your dog's status. For example, do not let him barge through the door in front of you. Tell him to "Wait" for you to go first, and then call him through.

TOY TANTRUMS

- If your dog is becoming possessive over toys, make sure you do not leave any toys lying around the place.
- Keep toys out of reach, and only produce one when you are training or during a play session. At the end of the session, take the toy back.

This will teach the dog that you have control of the toys, and he can play with them only when you give permission.

PERSONAL SPACE

Some dogs become resentful if you invade their personal space, and do not want to be disturbed when they are in their bed/indoor kennel.

- If this happens, you may make better progress if you put the indoor kennel out of bounds until you have overcome the problem. If your dog does not have a bed to use as a substitute, just put some bedding on the floor and he will be perfectly comfortable.
- When you approach the dog when he is in bed, offer him a treat, so that he learns to welcome you. Periodically, call the dog so that he gets out of his bed and comes to you. Then reward him with a treat.
- At other times, tell the dog to go to his bed.

Using these methods, you are controlling the dog's use of his sleeping quarters, and you have broken down his resentment if you come too close.

MEALTIME MANNERS

Food can become an issue if a dog is becoming too assertive. The dog tends to guard his food bowl, and growls if you interfere while he is eating.

- If this happens, drop some treats into the bowl while he is eating. Your dog will quickly learn to welcome your interference.
- When you see a noticeable improvement, you can take the bowl away halfway through the meal, tell the dog to "Wait", and then put it down again.
- Obviously you do not want to tease the dog at mealtimes, and once you are confident that your dog has accepted that you have control of his food bowl, you can leave him to eat in peace.

DOG AGGRESSION

If your dog has a sound temperament, aggression with other dogs is unlikely to be a deep-seated

Sometimes an adolescent dog will deliberately thwart house rules.

Arrange to meet up with a dog of impeccable temperament, so that you can set up a training situation.

When your dog focuses on his new companion, call him back to you, using a treat or a toy, and praise him lavishly when he responds.

problem. It is more likely to be a try on, as the dog comes to terms with his new maturity.

- Socialise your dog with one that will not be provoked (see page 115). Start off with both dogs on the lead, but keep the leads slack. Tension on the lead will make a dog more hyped up.
- Distract your dog with a treat or a toy so that he is still listening to you, and then let him go back to the other dog.
- Now walk the two dogs together, working at keeping your dog's attention on you.
- You may need to repeat this exercise on a number of occasions, but when you are ready, take the leads off and allow the dogs to interact. Hopefully, by this time, your dog has got over his excitement, and will play without showing any aggression.
- If you are worried about your dog biting, you can put a muzzle on him. This will mean that you are more relaxed when you are handling him, as you will be confident that he cannot inflict any damage.
- Do not avoid situations where you will meet other dogs. It is far better to address the problem rather than trying to limit opportunities. Go to a training class, so that your dog will meet other dogs in a controlled, working environment.

INTERRUPTING BEHAVIOUR

There are times when you want to halt inappropriate behaviour without coming down on the dog like a ton of bricks. You want to stop the behaviour, and then redirect him with a positive command. Training discs (which are like miniature cymbals) are specifically designed for this purpose.

Stand where your dog cannot see you, and, at the first sign of inappropriate behaviour, throw down the discs. The noise is enough to halt the dog in his tracks. He stops what he is doing to find out where the noise has come from. At that moment, you can call the dog back to you and reward him with a treat.

Training discs can be used in a number of different situations – for example, stopping a dog from barking excessively, halting a dog who is intent on raiding the bin, or putting a stop to play-biting. If you cannot get hold of training discs, a tin filled with pebbles will work equally well. The aim is to make a loud, sudden noise which the dog does not associate directly with you. The result is the dog stops what he is doing, without direct confrontation, and you can then be on hand to give a positive command and then praise him.

As with clicker training (see page 71), timing is all important, and you may need to seek guidance from an experienced trainer.

ATTENTION-SEEKING

A balanced relationship with a dog should be divided between quality periods of interaction, and times when the dog is content to settle and be self-sufficient. Some dogs are more needy than others, and become too dependent on human company. This behaviour can be expressed in a number of different ways:

• The dog tries to keep you in sight always, so that he is distressed even if you go to the bathroom!

• The dog seeks constant attention, nudging you to pet him at every opportunity. He may even bark in a bid to get your attention.

• The worst aspect of this problem is the dog that cannot be left on his own. A dog that is suffering from separation anxiety may bark or whine continuously when he is left. In its more severe form, the dog may be destructive or may foul the area he has been left in.

TRAINING STRATEGY

Debbie Coke is currently puppy walking her sixth dog, a German Shepherd called Timber. All but one of her puppies have qualified as guide dogs, and the dog she had just before Timber, a German Shepherd called Zara, is now in the final stages of training.

"I am rather smitten with German Shepherds," said Debbie. "They are so attentive and so quick to learn – their intelligence is spot on. Timber is only five months at the moment, but really I cannot fault him."

Debbie has three children, aged 15, 13 and 11, and puppy walking is very much a family affair.

"The children are so used to having puppies that they know exactly what to do and what not to do. I always get one of the kids to feed the puppy so that it does not become too attached to one person."

Debbie has had a few training problems to overcome with her puppies, and she has generally found that hard work and patience pays off.

"Zara was terrible for mouthing. There was nothing nasty in it, but it was a problem, particularly with the children. We worked on her right from the start, but it was habit that continued into adolescence.

"Then our puppy walking supervisor came up with a very effective solution. She had a can of pebbles, and positioned herself where the dog could not see her. When Zara went to mouth one of the children, she dropped the can. It made such a noise that Zara got a real shock. We only had to do it a couple more times, and Zara stopped mouthing altogether."

Guide Dog puppy Zara: Interrupting undesirable behaviour proved to be a quick and effective solution.

ACTION PLAN

It is a relatively small step from having a dog that is needy for human company to having a dog that cannot cope on his own. It is a nightmare for you if you cannot leave your dog, but equally, it is miserable for the dog, who suffers real distress when he is left. If you see signs of over-dependency, you must work at building your dog's confidence so that he learns to be self-sufficient.

HEALTHY NEGLECT

Your dog must learn that you are not there for him every minute of the day (or night).

- Work at the Settle exercise (see page 88). The dog is with you, but he will learn to lie quietly without seeking your attention.
- If the dog tries to paw at you, or barks to get your attention, ignore him. Withdraw eye contact and turn your back on him. The moment the dog is quiet, praise him. In this way, he will learn that barking and pawing gets him nowhere – being quiet gets him the attention he wants.

INDOOR KENNEL TRAINING

If you do not have an indoor kennel, now is the time to invest in one, as it will be invaluable in overcoming separation anxiety.

- Make the indoor kennel as inviting as possible with cosy bedding. Provide a boredom-busting toy, which can be stuffed with food treats. The dog has to work hard to get at the treats, and so he has something to occupy his mind.
- To begin with, confine the dog in his indoor kennel for a limited period, and stay in the same room. Hopefully, he will get stuck into his boredom-busting toy, and will be quite happy because you are in the same room.
- Graduate to going out of the room for a few minutes and then returning. Do not immediately release the dog when you return. Wait a few minutes, and then let him out in a matter-of-fact way. Do not go overboard with praise; it is important to keep things as low-key as possible.
- Gradually build up the time you can leave your

It is important to train your pup not to become too dependent on human company.

dog. If he barks or whines in protest, ignore him. It is essential that the dog learns that this behaviour is not rewarded. You may think you are rushing in to tell the dog off, but as far as he is concerned, he has got what he wanted – attention.
- Make a few mock departures, putting on your coat, jangling the car keys, and banging the front door. Wait for a limited period before returning to the dog. Again, keep the praise low-key. The aim is to take all the tension out of your comings and goings so the dog does not become anxious as you prepare to leave or wild with excitement when you return.
- You are now ready to leave your dog at home for a short time. Make sure you do not make a big production of it because you know that this time it is for real. Be matter-of-fact when you go, and when you return, delay a few minutes before going to release the dog.

If you work at the above exercises, your dog will gradually learn that he can be left on his own without major trauma. The advantage of using an indoor kennel is that the dog is confined and so he cannot be destructive. He is also highly unlikely to foul the area he is confined in.

You can also use a stair-gate to keep the dog in one room while you are in another. The dog will be able to see you and to hear you, but he will be learning to cope without being in your immediate presence.

BROADENING HORIZONS

Providing mental stimulation is the key to having a happy, healthy dog who relates well to you and your family. Obviously a dog will enjoy the physical exercise you give him, but mental exercise is just as important.

When Guide Dog puppies are around 12 months of age, they are ready to start their specialised training. From that point onwards, their lives will be busy and challenging.

For pet dogs, the exact opposite can be true. Many owners work hard at training and socialising, and when the dog has reached an acceptable level of obedience, they give up, satisfied that their job is done. The dog is well cared for, but he is missing out on the quality interaction he has had during his training. His brain is not stimulated, and his world has become narrower because he is no longer taken on outings for socialisation. Try to guard against this, and consider the following options for keeping your dog's brain and body active:

TIME TO SETTLE

Pippa was the first of Julie's dogs to enter training.

J ulie Griffiths is currently puppy walking her fifth Guide Dog puppy, an 11-week black Labrador called Jacob. The other breeds she has walked include a Labrador-Curly Coat cross, a Labrador-Retriever cross and a Flat Coat Retriever.

"I love the Retriever breeds," said Julie. "They are so friendly and so placid. The pup I've got at the moment does get excited, but he doesn't get hyped up."

One of the reasons why Julie and her family opted to be puppy walkers is because they knew the puppies they would get would be sound and reliable in temperament.

"The work that goes into the breeding programme means that there is a certain type of dog that you are likely to get. Of course, they are individuals, but they mostly share a calm attitude and nothing much bothers them."

Julie socialises her puppies in shops and restaurants, and she takes them on buses and on trains.

"I try to expose them to as many different environments as possible because you don't know where they will be working as guide dogs. I remember

OUT AND ABOUT

When you are going out, take your dog with you – unless there is a good reason why this is not possible. If you are walking to the shop to buy a newspaper, or driving into town, take the dog with you. He will appreciate the change of scene, no matter how mundane it appears to you, and he will enjoy being part of the family's activities.

BASIC TRAINING

Repeat basic training exercises now and again. This will sharpen up your dog's responses, and it will also give you the opportunity to praise and reward him.

HAVING FUN

Set aside time to play with your dog – retrieve is a

When Guide Dog puppies are around 12 months of age they start their formal training.

taking one of the pups to a fairground, where there were lots of different sights and sounds to get used to."

The only big problem Julie has had to overcome was when her second Guide Dog puppy, Bianca refused to settle on her own.

"To be honest, it was my own fault," said Julie. "I got Bianca a couple of weeks before my first puppy, Pippa, went into training. I let the two dogs sleep together, and then when Pippa went, Bianca wouldn't settle. She howled all through the night, and it got so bad that I had to sleep next to her on the sofa otherwise no one would have had any sleep."

Julie solved the problem by gradually building up the length of time she could leave Bianca.

"I had a stair-gate across the kitchen door, and I put Bianca on one side of it so she could still see me. She used to lie alongside the stair-gate, and, after a while, she would go to sleep. I would then go upstairs and leave her until she woke up. I let her cry for a few minutes, and then went down to her. Gradually, I could leave her for longer and longer periods while I was in the house. Then I started to build up the length of time I could leave her when I had to go out.

"By the time she went into training, she was fine. She had no problems whatsoever about being left on her own."

Julie admits that she finds it hard when it is time for a puppy to go in for training.

"But when you get the photo showing the dog you have puppy walked with its new owner, it is all worthwhile. You look at that photo, and you think: 'I helped to make this happen', and it really is a wonderful feeling."

Julie's second puppy, Bianca, found it hard to settle when Pippa went in for training.

great game to choose, as it combines physical and mental exercise. You could also try teaching your dog some fun tricks, such as giving his paw, begging, or rolling over on command. The dog will be stimulated by learning something new, and he will enjoy showing off his party piece when visitors come round.

GOOD CITIZEN AWARDS

Ensure that your dog has impeccable manners. If you have not already done so, find a dog-training club that runs the Good Citizen Award Scheme, and work towards getting your Gold Award (see page 95).

COMPETITIVE OBEDIENCE

If you get bitten by the training bug, and your dog shows a real aptitude, you may want to have a go at Competitive Obedience. You will need to find a club that specialises in this discipline so that you can be taught all the exercises that are required. They include:

- Heelwork (on and off the lead, at different paces).
- Stays (including out of sight).
- Recalls (calling the dog to you when you are standing still or when you are on the move).
- Retrieve (a dumb-bell, graduating to any article of the judge's choice).
- Sendaway (sending the dog to a fixed point where he must lie down).
- Distance control (putting the dog into the Sit,

If you and your dog have enjoyed basic training, you may like to give Competitive Obedience a go.

Stand, and Down from a distance).
- Scent discrimination (the dog has to find a scent cloth marked with your scent or the judge's scent).

AGILITY

This is a fast-moving sport where both dogs and handlers need to be fit. You will have to wait until your dog is 12 months of age before starting Agility training, and then you will need to find a specialist club. Dogs of all sizes are eligible, as the height of the obstacles is lowered for the 'minis'.

The aim of an Agility competition is to complete an obstacle course in the fastest time. Time faults are added if the dog takes the wrong course, knocks down a pole, or misses a contact point (on/off points of the A-frame, the dog walk, and the seesaw). The obstacles include:
- Hurdles (lowered for the mini breeds).
- Tunnels (rigid or collapsible).
- Weaves (a series of the poles through which the dog must weave).
- Tyres (lollipop or in a frame, lowered for the minis).
- A-frame (an 'A'-shaped structure where the dog must climb on and off, hitting the contact points).
- Dog walk (a narrow plank sloping up, along a

Agility is a fun sport for dog and owner.

Working Trials combines control, agility and tracking.

Freestyle is becoming an increasingly popular discipline.

straight line, and sloping downwards, with on/off contact points).

- Seesaw (with on/off contact points).
- Table/pause box (where the dog must go into the Down for a limited period).
- Long jump (reduced for the minis).

WORKING TRIALS

This is a challenging sport where the dog must have a good nose, as tracking forms a major part of the work. The other elements involved are control, which tests a dog's obedience, and agility. The Working Trials Stakes are progressively more difficult. For example, the Companion Dog (CD) Stake involves the following:

- Heelwork on and off the lead.
- Recall.
- Sendaway.
- Two-minute Sit.
- Ten-minute Down.
- Clear jump (an upright hurdle).
- Long jump.
- Scale (a solid upright obstacle, which the dog must negotiate in combination with a Stay and a

Recall).
- Retrieve (a dumb-bell).
- Elementary search.

The ultimate aim in Working Trials is the Patrol Dog Stake. This tests the dog's advanced control, agility and tracking, as well as a category on searching for criminals. It includes:

- Quartering the ground.
- Test of courage.
- Search and escort.
- Recall from criminal.
- Pursuit and detention of criminal.

CANINE FREESTYLE

In complete contrast, you may like to have a go at dancing with your dog! This is a new innovation, which is catching on fast. It involves teaching the dog a number of moves, piecing them together and setting them to music. To excel in this discipline, both you and your dog need to be real showmen! There are a limited number of clubs that teach Canine Freestyle, or you may need to find a personal trainer.

A dog thrives on having plenty to do and spending quality time with his human family.

LAST WORDS

It does not matter what you do with your dog – as long as you do something! A fun trick performed at home can be just as rewarding for you and your dog as being successful in a competition.

Some dogs and owners thrive on the pressure of competing, whereas others may prefer a more low-key approach. As long as the dog has an active, varied life, has a chance to use his brain, and can spend quality time with his family, he will be the happiest, healthiest and most contented dog in the world.